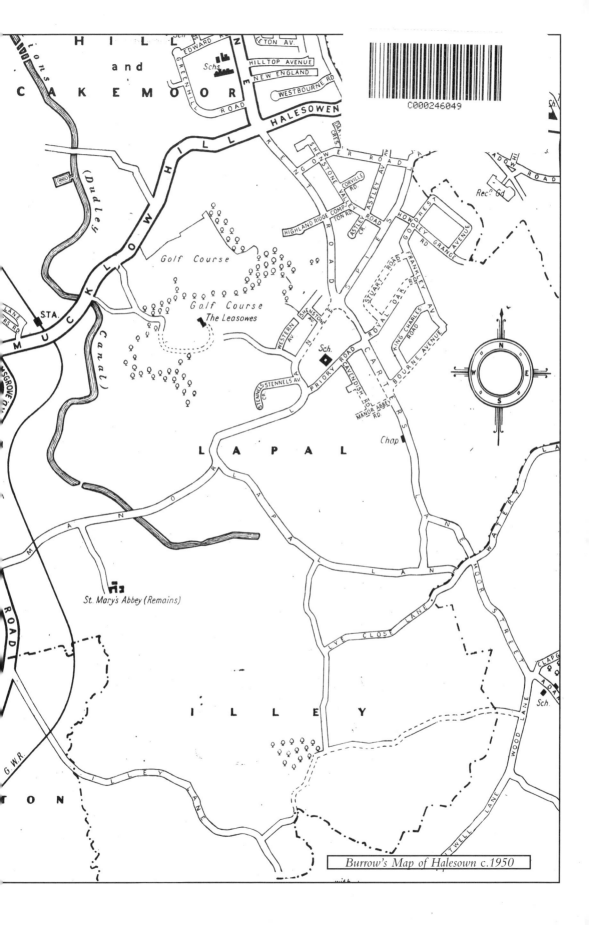

Burrow's Map of Halesown c.1950

A HISTORY OF
HALESOWEN

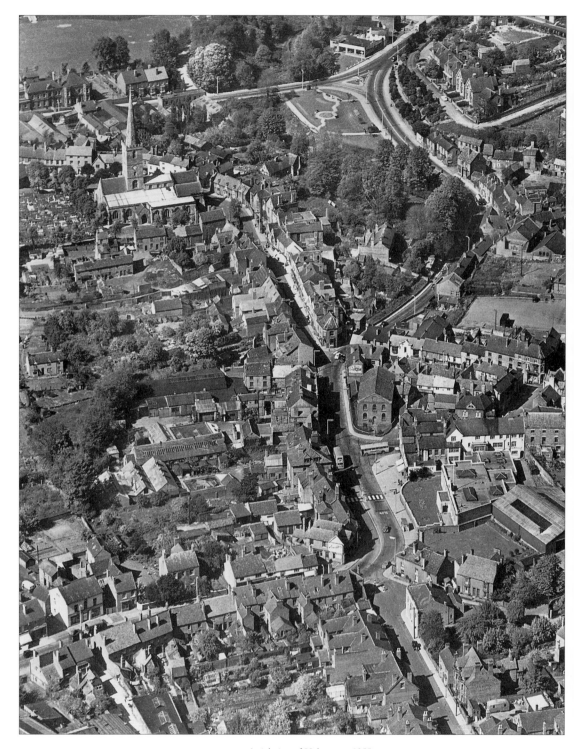

Aerial view of Halesowen, 1955

A HISTORY OF
HALESOWEN

Julian Hunt

With a foreword by David Eades
and line drawings by Bill Hazlehurst

Phillimore

2004

Published by
PHILLIMORE & CO. LTD
Shopwyke Manor Barn, Chichester, West Sussex, England

ISBN 1 86077 317 6

Printed and bound in Great Britain by
MPG BOOKS
Bodmin, Cornwall

CONTENTS

✧

LIST OF ILLUSTRATIONS

෴

vii

ACKNOWLEDGEMENTS

My father, Joseph Hunt, has always been fascinated with the history of Halesowen and has a particular interest in Halesowen Abbey. He has made available all his archives and notes and given me constant encouragement in writing this book. David Eades, author of two earlier books on Halesowen, has also shared with me the fruits of many years' research, and introduced me to many knowledgeable friends. He has loaned many of the photographs included in the book, several taken to illustrate his thesis on Education in Halesowen, prepared in 1966. His photographs are numbered 5, 69, 81, 91, 94, 99, 112, 115-6 and 119-22.

Jill Guest, of Cradley Library, has kindly allowed me access to the photographs of Frank Beasley, who worked for Halesowen Borough Treasurer's Department in the 1950s and recorded many buildings that have since been demolished. Frank Beasley's photographs are 31, 33, 36-8, 42-3, 46, 50-1, 53, 57, 59-60, 62, 64, 72, 74, 77, 82, 102, 104 and 136. Angela Horton and the staff of Halesowen Library have been extremely helpful and allowed me to select from their excellent collection of local photographs. Those from Halesowen Library are numbered 3, 7, 9, 13, 15, 18-20, 22-5, 29, 34, 41, 47-8, 54, 61, 63, 67, 71, 73, 78, 83-5, 87, 101, 110, 117, 123, 126, 132-3, 135, 145-6, 148-9 and 151. The following institutions and individuals have contributed illustrations: the Royal Commission on Historical Monuments at Swindon, numbers 21, 39, 68, 97-8, 106 and 109; Worcestershire Record Office, numbers 14, 17, 76 and 100; Judith Green, numbers 11, 79, 86, 107 and 113; Muriel Harper, numbers 16, 26, 58, 140 and 142-3; Peter Barnsley, numbers 75 and 118; Jean Granger, numbers 55 and 105; Mrs G. Limb, numbers 89-90; Mike Dancer, number 70; Andrew Hollis, number 152; Phil Waldron, number 45 and Barry Willetts, number 138.

Permission to publish original drawings came from Arthur T. Lockwood for the book jacket, and from Lena Schwarz for the drawing of Bundle Hill House by her late husband, Hans Schwarz. Simmons Aerofilms gave permission to reproduce the aerial view used as the frontispiece. Others who gave help and encouragement include Helen Brady, Mary Holder, Jackie Kendall, Alan Petford, Eric Price and Peter Ward. The staff of Birmingham City Archives, Dudley Archives, Worcestershire Record Office and Dudley Metropolitan Borough Legal Services Department produced from their stores many of the deed parcels, rate books and rentals on which the histories of individual properties are based. Bernard Engle and Partners kindly sent photocopies from their archive.

I am particularly indebted to Bill Hazlehurst, who prepared the drawings of Great Cornbow, Hagley Street, High Street and Peckingham Street, recording each building as it was before the redevelopment of the 1960s. I know of no similar architectural record of an English market town. I would also like to pay tribute to the late Ella Johnson, an inspiring teacher, who made my years at Tenter Street School so memorable.

FOREWORD

❧❧

In 1854 John Noake wrote of Halesowen: 'The town abounds with curious specimens of half-timbered houses ... which contrast most favourably with the dingy, flat brick walls of some modern edifices, among which a Zion chapel rears its plain but untasteful proportions.' I wonder what he would write today? All except one of the half-timbered houses have gone, and most of the then modern edifices have also disappeared, except, of course, the Zion chapel, which today is a listed building; concrete abounds. How things change. Oh for a return to those far off days when Halesowen was in Worcestershire, the town setting was rural, and the pace of life was much slower. But am I looking at the past through rose-coloured spectacles?

Historians by their very nature look backwards to try to understand the present. However picturesque rural Halesowen appeared to be, life was not always idyllic, especially for the working classes (among whom were my family). My friend Julian Hunt has worked on his research for this book with great enthusiasm, and has approached it in a different way from the previous authors of the subject. He and I were growing up when the town was changing under the 1960s redevelopment so we have drawn on our early memories, and those of older people, to recreate the town as it was, and then trace the history of people and buildings through contemporary records. Many old Halesowen names have surfaced and on reading the forthcoming pages many memories will be rekindled, but present-day youngsters will have to use their imaginations to see streets and buildings which are no longer there. Bill Hazlehurst's artistry will be a great help here.

Halesowen has a fascinating history, and it would be easy to write the story of the town's growth from the perspective only of those who held high office in the town. Julian Hunt has combined that with an account of the lives of ordinary people, charting the changes in the buildings, as impressive town houses became shops and the town centre was gradually pedestrianised. One sees here, too, how the families intermarried, the story of the development of education in the borough. One fact that shines through very clearly is that there was a great deal of civic pride in the town, which reached its zenith on 15 September 1936 when the town was presented with its Charter of Incorporation, turning Halesowen Urban District into Halesowen Municipal Borough. Our political overlords thought that it would be better for that status to be removed and Halesowen was included in a much larger

Authority on 1 April 1974. For 80 years Halesowen had been an independent local authority within Worcestershire. Thirty years have now passed since it has been a small part of a large Metropolitan Borough. Times change and we change, and no one can be a King Canute, but you the reader must be the judge as you compare today with former times. You may feel the jury is still out, but, in civic pride, I feel the jury has cast its verdict. I commend this book to you, because I know you will enjoy it.

DAVID L. EADES

Halesowen, June 2004

Chapter I

LANDLORDS AND TENANTS

❧

Halesowen is situated in the north-east corner of Worcestershire, where the River Stour forms the northern boundary of both the parish and the county. Before the manor became the property of David ap Owen in the 12th century, it was known simply as 'Hales'. The literal meaning of this place-name element is 'a corner', but it usually describes a remote valley, or recess in a hill. The name Hales would therefore be appropriate for the Borough of Halesowen, or for the hamlet of Halen (now Hawne), from which the borough was probably detached in the 13th century. The place-name hardly describes the wider parish of Halesowen, however, which was once a heavily wooded, upland area of 12,000 acres divided into 14 agricultural units or hamlets. The hamlets of Cradley and Lutley, and part of Warley, were detached from the main manor well before the Norman Conquest. By 1086, the date of Domesday Book, William the Conqueror had given the remainder of the manor of

1 *Halesowen from the Leasowes, c.1790, showing the prominent position of the parish church, which was visible from many of the surrounding hamlets.*

Hales to Roger of Montgomery. It would then have included 11 hamlets: Romsley, Hunnington, Illey, Lapal, Hasbury, Hawne, Hill, Cakemore, Ridgacre, Oldbury and the remainder of Warley. For his own convenience Roger of Montgomery, as Earl of Shrewsbury, had the manor of Hales removed from Worcestershire and administered thereafter as part of Shropshire. Halesowen remained a detached part of Shropshire until 1844, when it was reunited with Worcestershire.

Halesowen in Domesday Book

Before the Conquest, the Saxon lord of the manor of Hales, a man named Olwine, drew his income not only from his tenants' rents and labour, but also from a house in Worcester and a saltpan in Droitwich. One of Olwine's predecessors probably acquired the Worcester property as part of a royal policy to fortify and enrich the county town by obliging all manors to place dependable men there. They would defend the city in time of war and contribute to its economic development in peacetime. A similar process would ensure the prosperity of the new borough established to exploit the salt-bearing waters of Droitwich.

Some light is thrown on such arrangements by the Burghal Hideage, a document compiled around 914, which lists the fortified towns of England vital to the campaign against the Danes. The Burghal Hideage reckoned that Worcester would need 1,200 hides for its defence. The hide was a taxable unit of arable land, perhaps 120 acres, or as much as one family could maintain. The compiler of the Burghal Hideage assumed that each hide in the county would provide one man and that 160 men could defend a furlong (220 yards) of a town's wall. Worcester's allocation of 1,200 hides therefore suggests perimeter defences of about a mile.

The system of taxation which underlies the Burghal Hideage was still in place when Domesday Book was compiled 150 years later. Here the duty to pay Worcestershire's 1,200 hides was divided between 12 'hundreds', which were groups of manors that together paid 100 hides. No fewer than seven of these hundreds belonged to the church: three to the Bishop of Worcester, two to the Abbot of Westminster, and one each to the Abbots of Pershore and Evesham. The manor of Hales was in the Hundred of Clent, and was taxed on 10 hides of land. This compares with nine hides for Clent itself, five and a half hides for Hagley, and three hides each for Oldswinford and Pedmore. By 1086, these tax assessments were out of date, for, as we shall see, there were great discrepancies between the rating and the actual value of these manors.

The Domesday Book entry for the manor of Hales tells us that four ploughs were employed on the demesne (home farm). It is likely that an agent ran the manor of Hales on Roger of Montgomery's behalf and farmed the demesne himself. The remainder of the land was cultivated by 36 villagers, 18 smallholders, four riders

2 *St John's Church, Halesowen, from the Finger Post, c.1950. Domesday Book records that there was a church with two priests in Halesowen in 1086.*

(possibly holding land on special terms) and two priests, with 41 ploughs between them. There were also eight serfs (farm servants), and two bondwomen (probably female farm servants). There was a separate one-and-a-half-hide estate within the manor where 'Roger the Huntsman' had one plough and six tenant farmers, and five smallholders had five ploughs. Woodland for hunting was much prized by the new Norman landlords and no doubt Roger the Huntsman would have kept a hunting lodge in readiness, should Earl Roger wish to enjoy the pleasures of the chase. This un-named estate may well be Romsley, which maintained a separate manor court and where hundreds of acres of woodland have survived to this day.

A comparison with the entry for Clent, presumably the meeting point for the Hundred, shows just how prosperous and populous Halesowen was in 1086. Before the Conquest, Clent had belonged to King Edward, so it naturally descended to King William. It was rated at nine hides, nearly as many as Halesowen, but the King's home farm only employed one-and-a-half ploughs (probably meaning 12 oxen, with eight to a plough). Clent had only 12 villagers and three smallholders who used a further nine-and-a-half-ploughs. There were also three 'oxmen'. This gives Clent a total agricultural workforce of 18, and only 11 ploughs, compared with 81 people in Halesowen employing 51½ ploughs. In one respect Clent appears to have had an extra resource in the form of two leagues of woodland. Perhaps, however, there was no need to measure Halesowen's woodland because the presence of a huntsman assumed a hunting forest. It is clear from these returns that the respective tax assessments of the two manors were ancient and that they had not been adjusted to keep pace with the economic development of Halesowen.

Halesowen seems even more prosperous if figures are added from the three sub-manors which were separately listed in Domesday Book. Cradley and part of Warley had evidently been granted to independent Saxon landlords before the Conquest. By 1086 they were in the hands of William Fitz Ansculf, whose base was Dudley

3 *Lutley Grange, 1974. The hamlet of Lutley had been detached from the manor of Halesowen before the Conquest and given as an endowment to the important church of Wolverhampton. The dean of Wolverhampton would have an agent living at Lutley Grange to collect his rents and run the home farm.*

Castle and whose lands included Frankley, Northfield, Selly Oak, Oldswinford, Pedmore, Hagley, Churchill and Belbroughton. The grant of such a large swathe of property around Halesowen to the holder of Dudley Castle was the basis for the competition between the towns of Halesowen and Dudley, and for the rivalry between their respective proprietors, the Lyttelton and Dudley families, which was maintained until the 20th century. In 1086, despite being rated at only one hide, Cradley already had four tenant farmers and 11 smallholders, using seven ploughs. Warley was rated at only half a hide, with two tenant farmers, eight smallholders and two farm servants, using five-and-a-half ploughs. The hamlet of Lutley had been given to the Collegiate Church of Wolverhampton before the Conquest. The land there was cultivated by two tenant farmers, one smallholder and two farm servants, with four ploughs between them.

If we add the figures from Cradley, Warley and Lutley to those of Halesowen, we get a total agricultural workforce of 111, employing 68 ploughs. These numbers began to rival those of Bromsgrove and Kidderminster and suggest that, by 1086, there might already have been a market in the hamlet of Halen or Hawne, serving Halesowen's 13 other hamlets. The parish church, serving a very wide geographical area and employing two priests, must have been an old Saxon foundation.

The Legend of St Kenelm

The presence of a huntsman at Halesowen in 1086 ties in well with the legend of St Kenelm, son of Kenulf, King of Mercia, who was reputedly murdered whilst hunting in the forest near Clent. The legend suggests that Quendrith, daughter of Kenulf, had the seven-year-old Kenelm killed by his tutor, Askebert, in order to secure her own succession to the throne of Mercia. Kenelm is indeed a genuine historical figure, for his signature appears as a witness to several Mercian charters. In 799 he signed a charter as Kenelm, son of Kenulf. He probably died before his father as his name does not appear after 812. It is entirely likely that the medieval monks who compiled lives of the saints combined an account of the struggle for power when Kenulf died in 821 with the story of the mysterious death of a member of the royal household in a hunting accident. The earliest manuscripts which recount the life of St Kenelm are contemporary with Domesday Book and specifically mention Clent as the place of his murder.

Despite its doubtful origin, the legend of St Kenelm caught the public imagination. A shrine was erected on the boundary of Clent and the hamlet of Romsley at the supposed site of the murder, and pilgrims came to the place seeking the forgiveness of sins and healing of ailments. The immediate area became known as Kenelmstowe ('stowe' meaning a place of importance). The Abbot of Halesowen exploited the legend in 1223 by moving the date of Halesowen's annual fair to the Feast of St Kenelm (17 July). Roger de Somery, lord of the manor of Clent, obtained a royal charter in 1253 to hold a four-day fair at St Kenelm's, also starting on 17 July. Visitors to the remote spot were catered for at nearby farmhouses in Clent and Romsley. An inn named the *Red Cow* stood on the site of the present-day St Kenelm's Hall; the inn-sign recalled that part of the legend which claims that a cow left its pasture and marked the place of Kenelm's murder until the body was discovered and removed to the Mercian capital, Winchcombe. The shrine of St Kenelm became a chapel serving the inhabitants of the hamlet of Romsley.

Bishop Charles Lyttelton, writing his history of Hagley about 1735, stated that no trace remained of the hamlet of Kenelmstowe except the well at St Kenelm's (now indeed filled up), which was 'handsomely coped with stone and much resorted to both before and since the Reformation by the superstitious vulgar, for the cure of sore eyes and other maladies'. He imagined that the hamlet of Kenelmstowe 'continued to be well inhabited till the great road from Bromsgrove to Dudley (which anciently led directly through it) was changed and carried through the town of Hales'.[1] Bishop Lyttelton gives no date for the supposed diversion of the road through Kenelmstowe and his selective quotations from the court rolls of Halesowen and Clent tend to exaggerate the size of the hamlet.

Halesowen Abbey

Under feudal law, all land was let out by the king in return for military service. It could therefore revert to the king when a land owning family died out, or earned the king's displeasure. This explains how Henry II was able to give the manor of Hales to his sister Emma, who had married David, son of Owen, Prince of Wales, in 1174, which led to the name Halesowen. When David ap Owen died in 1204,

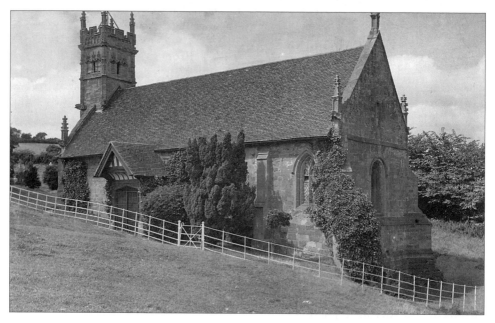

4   *St Kenelm's Church, built on the supposed site of the murder of Kenelm, prince of Mercia. The church is on the boundary of the parishes of Clent and Romsley.*

5 *The ruins of Halesowen Abbey, c.1910.*

the manor reverted to King John, who ten years later gave it to a powerful courtier, Peter des Roches, Bishop of Winchester, 'to build there a house of religion of whatever order he chooses'. The monks were, of course, to pray for the souls of King John and Peter des Roches. Only the greatest in the land had the prestige necessary to found a religious house, so King John was conferring a great honour on a faithful servant in providing the means with which Peter could endow an abbey. Peter des Roches chose the Premonstratensian order, deriving from Premontre in France and better known as the 'White Canons'. The first monks to set up their household at Halesowen came from the Premonstratensian Abbey of Welbeck, in Nottinghamshire.

The residents of Halesowen probably welcomed the arrival of the first Abbot, Roger of Joblington, who took up residence at Halesowen's manor house in 1218. He would have been in great need of food, building materials and labour, and the local economy would have been boosted by the market he established at Halesowen in 1220. The tenants' attitude to the Abbot would soon have changed, however, when he tried to maximise the Abbey's income by raising rents and demanding that the tenants work extra days on Abbey land. The wealthier farmers went to court claiming that they enjoyed ancient freedoms as tenants of King John, but the Abbot was able to show that Halesowen did not belong to the king at Domesday and that the charter setting up the Abbey in 1214 gave him every right to vary the customs of his manor. The records of the Abbot's court, where all land transactions and ordinances for regulating the common fields of Halesowen were registered, survive from 1270. There are some separate court rolls for the borough of Halesowen, and also for the hamlet of Romsley.[2]

The early Halesowen court rolls refer to many individuals whose surnames were derived from the location of their farmsteads, such as Hugh of Hasbury, Thomas of

6 *Medieval 'ridge and furrow' near Fieldhouse Farm, Romsley, 1998. The strips of land, or 'ridges', running down from Romsley Hill, were cultivated by separate farmers. Their leases obliged them to plough and harvest the crops on the Abbot of Hales' strips, which were intermingled with their own.*

Hill, Henry of Hunnington, Adam of Illey, John of Lapal and William of Romsley. Others had occupational surnames, including Richard Baker, Thomas Faber (smith), Nicolas Ironmonger, John Merchant, William Miller, Ralph Tanner and Thomas Tinctor (dyer). A few had names reflecting a family characteristic like Adam Snow, who was probably white-haired, or Thomas Squire, who enjoyed high status in the community. The court rolls also refer to familiar places such as the High Street and Cornbow, in the borough of Halesowen, Coombs Wood and the New Mill in Hill hamlet, the quarry and St Margaret's Well in Hasbury, the Waxlands in Hunnington and Uffmoor Wood and Dales Wood in Romsley.

Most of the Abbot's tenants held their farms for life, paying an annual rent, plus an entry fine recorded in the court rolls of the year they purchased or inherited their property. They were given a copy of the court roll as title to the land and were therefore called copyholders. A typical 30-acre farm, comprising upwards of 60 strips of land dispersed in three common arable fields, was called a virgate, or yardland. Rents were 3s. 4d. per yardland, with twice that sum paid as an entry fine. Smaller farms were half or quarter yardlands and paid proportionally less. Some smallholders or cottagers had landholdings of just one or two strips. Tenants could pasture their pigs in the woods and also take limited amounts of timber for house building and for fuel. The large trees were used for structural timber and pollarded trees for firewood. The Abbot would sell any surplus to timber merchants, or to the charcoal burners who supplied fuel for the local iron industry.

Each tenant was obliged to give up several days a year to cultivate the Abbot's own land, which was also scattered in strips in the open fields. In 1301, a yardland tenant called Thomas ate Laye was expected to spend three days ploughing, and three each harrowing and harvesting on the Abbot's land.[3] When a copyhold tenant died, his family had to pay the Abbot a heriot, usually the best beast in his herd. If a member of his family wanted to leave the manor, a fine was paid to the Abbot, and further fines were paid for permission to marry, or if a daughter bore an illegitimate child. The exact services the tenants owed to the Abbot and the rules governing the common arable fields were carefully recorded and were known as the customs of the manor. Copyholders are therefore called customary tenants in some accounts.

Corn Mills

Soon after the foundation of Halesowen Abbey, a manorial corn mill was erected on the Stour at the bottom of Mucklow Hill. The Abbot's tenants were required to grind their corn there rather than use hand mills or take their grain to a mill outside the parish. In 1278 the Abbot's bailiff intercepted a man coming from Frankley Mill with a sack full of flour and took it from him.[4] In 1280, Richard Melley was fined at the manor court for grinding his corn elsewhere than at the lord's mill.[5] The monopoly was deeply unpopular and, in 1293, the Abbot's new mill was burnt down.[6] The mill was rebuilt and continued to be the principal corn mill in the parish until its conversion into a slitting mill in the 18th century. When Hales Furnace was built downstream of the mill in the early 17th century, the occupant of Halesowen Mill was obliged to release sufficient water to power the furnace bellows. The miller would no doubt resent these terms. Thomas Beck was the occupant in 1670 when John Downing, the manager of Hales Furnace, himself took over the lease of the mill, probably to ensure a constant flow of water.[7] The mill pond, stretching back several hundred yards alongside Bromsgrove Road, was still known as the New Pool until it was drained and built over in the 1970s.

The Abbot of Halesowen built another corn mill at Shut Mill, in the hamlet of Romsley, and obliged his Romsley tenants to grind their corn there. A rental of the Abbey land in 1500 gives William Hall as the tenant of Shut Mill. The Hall family continued as millers there until at least 1690. In 1708 Thomas Palmer, agent to the lord of the manor, paid Isaac Brettell 10s. towards thatching Shut Mill and

7 *Grange Mill, Dogkennel Lane, c.1925. The farmers of Hunnington were probably encouraged by the lord of the manor to grind their corn here rather than at any rival mill.*

barn. The mill remained in production until the early 20th century. There was also the ancient Bird's Mill at Oldbury, and another on the Stour at Cradley. The date of Grange Mill, which must have served the tenants of Hunnington hamlet, is not known, but there is mention of a pool in the conveyance of the Grange to John Ive in 1558.[8] Other corn mills at Hayseech and Lutley were converted into gun-barrel boring mills in the 18th century.

The Common Fields

Each hamlet had two or more common arable fields, each covering hundreds of acres, which were communally ploughed, sewn and harvested at fixed times of the year. Each farmer within the hamlet would have a number of strips or ridges in each common field, so that all types of land, whether rich or barren, wet or dry, upland or lowland, were evenly distributed. Even if a farmer owned his own plough, he was unlikely to have the eight oxen required to pull it through the heavy soil. Farmers therefore contributed draft animals according to their means. The crop rotation system was employed in the hamlet of Hasbury: the farmers might grow a winter-sown crop of wheat on their strips in Witley Field (the field which gave its name to Witley Lodge, on Stourbridge Road); they would plant a spring-sown crop, perhaps peas or beans, on their strips in Huntingtree Field (the name now given to the *Huntingtree Inn* on Alexandra Road); the remaining field, the Highfield (to the west of Halesowen town centre) would be left fallow for pasturing their cattle. The next year, they would plant winter wheat on the Highfield, because it had been rested and nourished by the cattle dung. In the third year, they would plant wheat in Huntingtree Field, and so the three-year cycle of cropping was maintained. A 1558 lease of Porchhouse Farm to Ralph Harris listed his holdings in the three common fields of Hunnington in terms of the time it would take him to cultivate the land. He had 14 days' earth in Hannall Field, eight days' earth in Over Viccars Field and three days' earth in Nether Viccars Field. He also had seven leasowes, or pastures of enclosed land, probably taken out of the neighbouring woodland.[9]

The common fields of the borough of Halesowen were the New Field and the Tenter Field. The latter probably got its name from the clothiers' practice of hanging their cloth on tenters erected on their south-facing strips in the common field. There must have been a fulling mill serving the clothiers of Halesowen during the reign of Edward I, because Thomas the Skinner is recorded as drowning himself in the walkmill pool. The common fields of the hamlet of Hill were situated on the plateau at the top of Mucklow Hill. They were named Horslett Field and Tamworth Field. Most of Romsley's farms were situated on the north side of a row of common arable fields, that stretched from Romsley Hill in the east to Clent Hill in the west. In Nurfurrow Field, nearest to St Kenelm's, the strips ran north to south. Some of them, near to the modern Rectory, are still visible in a low morning sun. In Holloway Field, between Romsley Hill and Fieldhouse Lane, the surviving cultivation strips run east to west and are more obvious. The third field was called Broadway, where the strips ran south towards Shut Mill.

The Black Death

The plague of 1349, widely known as the Black Death, reduced the population of Halesowen by about one third. The priests who said mass for the dead were particularly vulnerable and it is perhaps significant that a new vicar, Roger de Hampton, was appointed in 1349. Some historians have suggested that Kenelmstowe, thought to have been an urban area next to St Kenelm's shrine at Romsley, disappeared as a result of the plague, but contemporary Halesowen court rolls show that whole communities were not wiped out and that most farms where the tenant had died were taken over by surviving relatives. Whilst some prominent families, like the Westleys of Romsley and the Lynacres of Hunnington, did succumb to the plague, other wealthy families, like the Squires of Romsley and the Gregorys of Hunnington, continued to farm there long after 1349.[10]

In the years following the plague, property and food prices fell dramatically and in many places landlords were forced to reduce or waive services in order to attract tenants. The Abbot of Halesowen faced organised opposition from tenants no longer willing to work the Abbey farmland as well as their own. Although the Abbot's right to demand labour services was upheld at an official enquiry into the customs of the manor in 1386,[11] he eventually gave up cultivating his own land. In 1396, the Abbot leased all his strips in the three common fields of Romsley to a group of tenants led by Thomas Squire.[12]

Enclosure of the Open Fields

The strips in the common arable fields of Halesowen were consolidated into private hedged enclosures earlier than those in most Midland parishes. This may have been the work of wealthy tenants such as Thomas Squire, who accumulated strips in a particular area and fenced them in, creating the hedged landscape we are familiar with today. Such enterprising tenants also paid the lord of the manor to let them cut down more woodland and extend their pasture. More conservative farmers saw these processes as a threat to their common rights and were inclined to destroy or burn the new fences.

The names of farms such as Newhouse and Fieldhouse in Romsley, Witley Lodge and Highfields in Hasbury, and Oatenfields and Dovehousefields in Hunnington suggest that they were built on former common fields. The Breach, a moated farm in Hunnington, appears to be ancient, yet its name means newly broken land. A remnant of the pre-enclosure landscape can be seen in the long, thin plots of land on the 1840s tithe maps, such as that attached to the Tithe Award for Hill, where some of the cultivated land near Long Lane remained in strips.

The Abbot of Halesowen had evidently allowed some enclosure of the common fields, for there was a complaint at the manor court in 1480 that William Locock of Romsley 'keeps in severalty closed one field called le middlefield, which certain field was accustomed to be open each third year, and all years after the grains are carried off'.[13] The speed of enclosure increased with the Dissolution of the Monasteries, when purchasers of former abbey lands sought a quick return on their investments.

8   *Oatenfields Farm, c.1910. The farm takes its name from the Oaten Field, one of the common arable fields of the hamlet of Hunnington.*

By buying and exchanging strips, the new owners could accumulate larger blocks of land. The hedges they planted around these new enclosures transformed the prairie-like medieval landscape into our modern landscape of small hedged fields.

Abbots of Hales Owen

Roger of Joblington 1218–	William of Bromsgrove 1366–1369
William	Richard of Hampton 1369–1391
Richard 1232–1245	John of Hampton 1391–1395
Henry of Branewyck	John Poole 1395–1422
Martin	Henry of Kidderminster 1422–
Nicholas	William Hemele
John 1298–1305	John Darby 1446–1486
Walter of the Flagge 1305–1314	Thomas Bruges 1486–1505
Bartholomew 1314–1322	Edmund Green 1505–
Thomas of Lech 1322–1331	William Taylor 1538–
Thomas of Birmingham 1331–1366	

The Dissolution of the Monasteries

Halesowen Abbey was dissolved in 1538. The last abbot, William Taylor, was given a handsome pension of £66 13s. 4d. for life. He may have continued as tenant of the Abbey lands, for the inventory attached to his will in 1545 lists considerable property in Halesowen. The other residents of Halesowen Abbey were also given pensions.

Pensions awarded to the inmates of Halesowen Abbey in 1538

William Taylor	£66 13s. 4d.	William Glasgar	£4 0s. 0d.
Nicholas Greeves	£10 0s. 0d.	Richard Gregory	£3 6s. 8d.
Robert Shyngfells	£6 0s. 0d.	Thomas Blunt	£2 13s. 4d.
Thomas Robinson	£6 0s. 0d.	Henry Cooke	£7 5s. 8d.
William Bolton	£4 0s. 0d.	[blank] Hawkesworth	£2 0s. 0d.
Alexander Whytehead	£5 0s. 0d.	Albert Stacey	£2 13s. 4d.
Will Boroden	£5 0s. 0d.	Thomas Singulton	£2 13s. 4d.
Joseph Rogers	£3 6s. 8d.	Thomas Blount	£2 6s. 8d.

In 1539, Henry VIII sold the manor of Halesowen and the site of the dissolved Abbey to a promising courtier named Sir John Dudley, who built up a large portfolio of former monastic property.[14] John Dudley had recently acquired Dudley Castle, having given a £2,000 mortgage to his namesake John Sutton, Lord Dudley, and taken possession when the sum could not be paid back. In 1539 Sir John Dudley wisely settled the manor of Halesowen on his wife, Joan, and their children. The site of the Abbey and the home farm was let in 1549 to Dudley's agent, George Tuckey. It is described in the lease as:

> the mansion of the manor of Hales, that is the hall, buttery, pantry, kitchen, all the chambers over and between them, the water chambers, the nursery houses, the laughton houses with the barn and cow house, the malthouse, mill and gardens, all the stables, the gatehouse under and over, the great tiled barn with one lesser tiled barn, and one ox house at the grange upon Uffmore, with all the houses builded upon Brackley Breache, with a tiled barn called Witley and all the little park there and all houses within the same, and also all orchards and gardens, with all the fields and pastures called Laphall Fields, Cotefield and Hayfield, with certain pastures and medows called the Brache lying in the township of Honyngton and within the pale of Uffmore, with one sling of meadow called Holme medowe, and also the conies within the said premises, except and only reserved all woods and underwoods growing in or upon the premises and all pools water and fishing in the same.[15]

Sir John Dudley was made Earl of Warwick in 1547, and was one of the executors of Henry VIII's will. Under Edward VI he became Duke of Northumberland and the strongest man in the government. When Edward VI was terminally ill in 1553, he persuaded the young king to make a will disinheriting his Catholic sister Mary, who, he feared, would reverse his religious policies and return monastic lands to the Church. The Crown was instead to pass to Edward VI's cousin, Lady Jane Grey, who had married Northumberland's son, Guildford Dudley. Queen Jane was crowned, but her reign lasted only nine days. Northumberland failed to capture Mary, and his supporters melted away. Mary was proclaimed Queen. Northumberland, his son Guildford and the unfortunate Jane were tried and executed. Northumberland's widow, Joan, appeared before the Court of Augmentations and successfully claimed the manor of Halesowen as her right under the 1539 family settlement. On her death in 1555 the manor passed with other properties to her three remaining sons, Ambrose, Henry and Robert, who

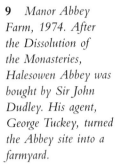

9 *Manor Abbey Farm, 1974. After the Dissolution of the Monasteries, Halesowen Abbey was bought by Sir John Dudley. His agent, George Tuckey, turned the Abbey site into a farmyard.*

had themselves been tried for treason, but had escaped with their lives. Robert Dudley, later to become Queen Elizabeth's favourite, bought out his brothers and, in 1558, sold the manor of Halesowen to George Tuckey and another local man, Thomas Blount, for £3,000.[16] This Thomas Blount may be the monk of the same name who was resident at Halesowen Abbey at the Dissolution. It is also worth noting that the sale did not include the township of Oldbury, which had been settled on Robert Dudley and his wife Amy Robsart. Oldbury continued as a separate manor, and was held by the Robsart family until 1633.

In 1558, the new owners of the manor of Halesowen, George Tuckey and Thomas Blount, offered the best farms to the sitting tenants on 1,000-year leases. The object of the long leases was probably to avoid excessive payments to the Court of Augmentations, which licensed sales of former monastic property. John Ive of Halesowen, yeoman, paid Blount and Tuckey £125 for 'All that their Mansion House situate and being near unto the Town of Halesowen aforesaid in the said County of Salop commonly called the Graunge', and undertook to pay them a rent of 12d. per year for 1,000 years. Ralph Harris of Hunnington, who leased Porchhouse Farm for 1,000 years, also paid 12d. rent. Similarly, Richard Harris of Romsley, who leased 'All that Capital Messuage called ye sign of the Cow in Romsley', agreed to pay 4d. rent per year for 1,000 years.[17]

Sir John Lyttelton (d.1589)

When, in 1558, Thomas Blount and George Tuckey had leased off as much of the manor of Halesowen as the market would stand, they sold the remainder, including the site of the dissolved Abbey, to Sir John Lyttelton.[18] The Lyttelton's principal estate, which they had held since the early 15th century, was at Frankley, but they also owned the manor of Arley, near Bewdley. The Lytteltons were typical of the Worcestershire gentry who adhered to the old religion throughout the upheavals of the 16th century. John Lyttelton married Bridget, daughter of Sir John Packington, whose house at Harvington contains many 'priest holes' and remains a shrine to Catholicism in the county. When Queen Mary came to the throne in 1553 Sir John Lyttelton was rewarded with the office of Constable of Dudley Castle, which had passed to the Crown with the execution of the Duke of Northumberland. Buying the manor of Halesowen did not completely exhaust the Lytteltons' resources, for John Lyttelton was able to purchase the neighbouring manors of Hagley and Cradley in 1565. Although a Catholic, he was accepted at Elizabeth's court and was knighted in 1566. Sir John Lyttelton died in 1589 and was succeeded by his eldest son Gilbert Lyttelton.

Gilbert Lyttelton (c.1540–99)

Gilbert Lyttelton, who inherited estates at Frankley, Halesowen and Hagley, was MP for Worcestershire in 1571 and High Sheriff of the county in 1584. He married Elizabeth, daughter of Humphrey Coningsby of Neen Sollars in Shropshire, but later became estranged from her and disputed his own children's inheritance. Gilbert was engaged in a long legal battle with Edward Lord Dudley over land and coal mines at Prestwood in Staffordshire. He died in 1599 and was buried at Frankley. His son, John Lyttelton, succeeded him.

John Lyttelton (1561–1601)

John Lyttelton was born in 1561. He was a student at Magdalen College, Oxford, in 1576 and at the Inner Temple in 1580. He represented Worcestershire in the Parliaments of 1584, 1586 and 1597 and was a party to his father's dispute with Edward Lord Dudley. He inherited the family estates in 1599, when there was no established successor to the ageing Queen Elizabeth and some Catholic families saw an opportunity to return England to the Catholic fold. John Lyttelton was implicated in Essex's rebellion in 1601 and convicted of treason. His life was spared, but he died in prison in July 1601 and his estates were forfeited to the Crown. Only four years later, his brother, Humphrey Lyttelton, and his cousin Stephen Lyttelton of Holbeach, near Stourbridge, were executed for their roles in the Gunpowder Plot. John Lyttelton had married Meriel, daughter of the Lord Chancellor, Sir Thomas Bromley, in 1590. After her husband's death, she successfully appealed for the restoration of the family estates, apparently on condition that she brought up her sons within the Church of England. She managed the estates prudently and her name appears on many sales and leases of the period, including a 1609 lease of the right to dig iron ore from Lord Dudley's land for use in her iron furnace at Halesowen. She was the first of the Lytteltons to make Hagley their principal residence.

Sir Thomas Lyttelton (1596-1649) 1st Bart.

Thomas Lyttelton was born in 1596, and studied at Balliol College, Oxford and at the Inner Temple. He was made a baronet by James I in 1618. He represented Worcester in Parliament from 1621-6, and again in 1640. On the outbreak of the Civil War, he raised a regiment of both horse and foot soldiers for the King. As governor of Bewdley, he was taken prisoner by Parliamentary forces in 1644 and fined £4,000 for his 'delinquency'. His house at Frankley was garrisoned by the Royalists, who burnt it down in 1644, ostensibly to prevent its being used by the enemy. There is no evidence that his property in Halesowen was attacked, so his tenants there were probably wise enough to surrender whatever resources were demanded by the Royalist garrison at Dudley or the Parliamentary garrison at Birmingham. Sir Thomas Lyttelton's most valuable and strategic possession was his iron furnace at Halesowen, which was probably leased to Richard Foley, the Stourbridge ironmaster. Foley could refine the pig iron produced there at any of his forges along the Stour, and could move the products down river to Worcester. There were regular orders from the King's armourer to Richard Foley, to deliver guns and ammunition to Worcester for shipment to Oxford. Sir Thomas Lyttelton died in 1649 and was buried in Worcester Cathedral. He was succeeded by his son, Henry Lyttelton.

Sir Henry Lyttelton (1624-93) 2nd Bart.

Sir Henry Lyttelton was born in 1624 and was a student at Balliol College, Oxford, in 1640. He was taken prisoner at the Battle of Worcester in 1651 and imprisoned in the Tower until 1653 on a charge of supplying arms without licence to the Scottish army. In 1659, he was implicated with two of his brothers in Sir George Booth's insurrection. He was again sent to the Tower but no evidence was given against him, two of his servants and John Wright, the schoolmaster from Halesowen, who could have testified, having disappeared. About 1675, Sir Henry Lyttelton increased the income of the curate at St Kenelm's Chapel by allotting the greater part of the tithes of Romsley to the curacy. He was MP for Lichfield from 1677-9. He died without issue in 1693 and was buried at Arley. He was succeeded by his brother Charles Lyttelton.

Sir Charles Lyttelton (1629-1716) 3rd Bart.

Charles Lyttelton was born in 1629, fought with the Royalists at the siege of Colchester in 1648 and escaped to France in 1650 where he became Cupbearer to Charles II. He too was involved in Sir George Booth's rising in 1659. Although a fervent royalist, he married Katherine, daughter of Sir William Fairfax, a member of the famous Yorkshire Parliamentary family. In 1662, Charles Lyttelton went to Jamaica as Lieutenant Governor. His wife died there. He then married Anne, daughter and co-heiress of Thomas Temple of Frankton, Warwickshire who was MP for Bewdley in 1685. He inherited the family estates on the death of his brother, Sir Henry Lyttelton, in 1693. He sold the freehold of the farm at Ridgacre to the copyhold tenant, Jacob Smith, in 1707.[19] He died at Hagley in 1716 and is buried at Upper Arley. He was succeeded by his fifth, and only surviving, son, Thomas Lyttelton.

Sir Thomas Lyttelton (1686-1751) 4th Bart.

Thomas Lyttelton was born in 1686 and inherited the Lyttelton estates in Worcestershire in 1716. He had already made a most advantageous marriage in 1708 to Christian, daughter of Sir Richard Temple of Stowe, in Buckinghamshire. Her brother, Richard Temple, was the founder of a highly successful political dynasty which included several of his Lyttelton relations. When Richard Temple became Viscount Cobham in 1718, the grant contained a special remainder to his sisters which was eventually to bring the title of Lord Cobham to the Lyttelton family. The fashion for landscape gardening was nowhere more lavishly realised than at Stowe, and the Lytteltons were soon to copy their Buckinghamshire cousins by enhancing their park at Hagley. Sir Thomas Lyttelton was MP for Worcestershire in 1727 and provided Halesowen's first workhouse in 1730. Three of his children were MPs and one a bishop. The eldest son, George (1709-73), became Chancellor of the Exchequer and was created Baron Lyttelton of Frankley; Charles Lyttelton (1714-68) became Bishop of Carlisle and was a noted antiquarian, his notes forming the basis of Nash's *History of Worcestershire*. Richard Lyttelton (1718-70) married the widow of the Duke of Bridgewater and through this connection became MP for Brackley in 1747. William Henry Lyttelton (1724-1808) was MP for Bewdley and was created Baron Lyttelton of Frankley after the original title had died out. Sir Thomas Lyttelton died in 1751 and was succeeded by his son George Lyttelton.

George, 1st Lord Lyttelton (1709-73)

George Lyttelton was born in 1709. He was a student at Christ Church, Oxford, in 1726 and went on the grand tour in 1728. In 1742 he married Lucy, daughter of Hugh Fortescue of Filleigh, Devon. The marriage settlement contains a long list of tenants in Halesowen whose farms and houses were to provide an income for their children. The couple had a son, Thomas, and a daughter, Lucy. George Lyttelton's wife died in 1747 and in 1749 he married Elizabeth, daughter of Sir Robert Rich Bart. George Lyttelton inherited Hagley and the other Worcestershire estates in 1751. His Parliamentary career began in 1735, when he was offered a seat at Okehampton by Viscount Cobham. He represented that town until he moved to the House of Lords in 1756. He rose to the position of Chancellor of the Exchequer in 1754, but contemporary commentators were rather critical of his financial abilities. His elevation to the peerage in 1756, as Baron Lyttelton of Frankley, was both a reward and an acknowledgement that he had no future in the Commons. In 1756 he began the rebuilding of Hagley Hall, advised by Sanderson Miller, a friend and amateur architect from Radway in Warwickshire. The style was Palladian and featured the prominent corner turrets fashionable at the time. The parish church of Hagley, which stands close by the house, was also remodelled. The park was

embellished by the building of a mock-
gothic castle using materials taken from
the ruins of Halesowen Abbey. The costs
of the rebuilding were partly shared by
George's brothers Richard, who had
married the Duchess of Bridgewater, and
Charles, then Bishop of Carlisle. George
Lord Lyttelton was much troubled by
the life style of his eldest son Thomas.
When Thomas Lyttelton left his wife
Apphia, soon after their marriage in
1772, she went to live at Hagley Hall
and remained there until George Lord
Lyttelton's death in 1773.

Thomas 2nd Lord Lyttelton (1744-79)

Thomas Lyttelton was born at Hagley
in 1744. He was a student at Christ
Church, Oxford, in 1761. He is often
styled 'wicked' Lord Lyttelton, as he
was a notorious gambler and womaniser,
and is said to have run through the

10   *George Lyttelton, created Lord Lyttelton
in 1756.*

family fortune. History's verdict should perhaps be more measured: his father
must have strained the family finances with the rebuilding of Hagley Hall, and
his inheritance in 1773 coincided with the slump in sales of timber for charcoal,
when local iron furnaces converted to the burning of coal. He was elected
MP for Bewdley in 1768 but was unseated on petition in 1769. In 1772, whilst
staying with his father at Hagley, Thomas Lyttelton met a rich widow called
Apphia Peach, who was then living at the Leasowes, formerly the home of the
poet Shenstone. She was the daughter of Broome Witts of Chipping Norton, and
widow of Joseph Peach, who had been Governor of Calcutta. The couple were
married at Halesowen before the marriage settlement had been signed. Thomas
Lyttelton therefore gained complete control of her fortune of £20,000. By the
time he inherited the Worcestershire estates on his father's death in 1773, Thomas
Lyttelton had left his wife and was living in Paris. In 1775 he was forced to sell
12 farms in Hasbury, Hill, Cakemore, Warley Wigorn, Warley Salop, Ridgacre,
Lapal, Illey and Romsley.[20] The sale of Romsley Hill Farm to John Durant, vicar
of Hagley, raised £800 alone. In 1779 he sold a further 87 acres of arable land
at Oatenfields, Hunnington, to Lord Dudley and Ward.[21] Thomas Lord Lyttelton
was even prepared to sell off his right to collect the tithes of Halesowen parish,
which his ancestor had purchased with the lands of Halesowen Abbey. He therefore
accepted lump sums from proprietors, such as Edward Horne of the Leasowes,

11   *Hagley Hall, rebuilt in the 1750s by Sanderson Miller for George Lord Lyttelton.*

whose estates were subsequently free of tithes.[22] Thomas Lord Lyttelton did not care for his father's new house at Hagley and preferred to live at his own home, Pitt Place in Epsom, which brought him much nearer to his London friends. He died at Pitt Place in 1779, having dreamed of his death three days beforehand. He had no children, so the Lyttelton peerage died with him. He was succeeded at Hagley by his uncle, William Henry Lyttelton, but he left Arley Hall to his sister Lucy, wife of Arthur Annesley, Viscount Valentia.

William Henry 1st Lord Lyttelton (1724–1808)

William Henry Lyttelton was born in 1724. He was a student at St Mary Hall, Oxford, in 1742 and at the Middle Temple in 1743. He was called to the bar in 1748 but chose instead to go into Parliament, representing Bewdley from 1748-55. He was Governor of South Carolina from 1755-60 and of Jamaica from 1760-6. He married Mary, daughter and coheir of James McCartney of Longford, Ireland in 1761. She died in 1765, but he married again in 1774, this time Caroline, daughter of John Bristowe of Quidenham, Norfolk. He represented Bewdley again from 1774-90 and was Lord of the Treasury from 1777-82. He was given an Irish peerage in 1776, as Baron Westcote of Ballymore, Co. Longford, and in 1794 he was created Baron Lyttelton of Frankley. He inherited Hagley and the Worcestershire estates on the death of his nephew, Thomas Lord Lyttelton, in 1779. He died in 1808 leaving Hagley to his son George Fulke Lyttelton.

George Fulke 2nd Lord Lyttelton (1763-1828)

George Fulke Lyttelton was born in Jamaica in 1763. He was a student at Balliol College, Oxford, in 1781. He succeeded his father as MP for Bewdley in 1790, but gave up the seat in 1796 in favour of a friend of the family. He seems to have been physically weak and also suffered from a mental illness. He died in 1828, when his brother William Henry Lyttelton succeeded to the title and estates.

William Henry 3rd Lord Lyttelton (1782-1837)

William Henry Lyttelton was born in 1782, he studied at Christ Church, Oxford, in 1798 and became a fine classical scholar. His advantageous marriage in 1813 to Sarah, daughter of George John, Earl Spencer, was no doubt made possible by the expectation that he would succeed his unmarried and invalid brother George as Lord Lyttelton. He was MP for Worcestershire from 1806-20, supporting reform and the abolition of the slave trade. He eventually succeeded to the title and the family estates on the death of his half-brother George in 1828. He himself died in 1837 at the house of his brother-in-law, the 3rd Earl Spencer, in Green Park. His widow Sarah lived until 1870 and became Lady of the Bedchamber to Queen Victoria, and Governess to the royal children.

George William 4th Lord Lyttelton (1817-76)

George William Lyttelton was born in 1817. At Eton he developed a love of cricket and at Trinity College, Cambridge, he became a distinguished classical scholar. He inherited the title of Lord Lyttelton in 1837 when only 20. He was appointed Lord Lieutenant of Worcestershire in 1839, a post which he held for life and which he took very seriously. That same year he married Mary, the younger daughter of Sir Stephen Glynne of Hawarden. It was a double wedding for, on the same day, her elder sister, Catherine, married William Gladstone. The brothers-in-law shared a love of the classics and a belief in high church principles. George Lord Lyttelton was responsible for the restoration of St Kenelm's, Romsley, in 1846, and the east window was donated by Gladstone. When the rector of Hagley died in 1846, George Lord Lyttelton was able to appoint his younger brother, William Henry Lyttelton, to the Rectory. In 1857, the brothers rebuilt Hagley Church in the prevailing gothic style, and were also responsible for the addition of its incongruous steeple in 1865. It was through his high church connections that George Lord Lyttelton became a key supporter of the settlement of Canterbury in New Zealand, underwriting some of the costs and visiting the colony in 1867. Whilst William Gladstone had a glittering political career, George Lord Lyttelton failed to make a mark in politics, apart from a brief period as Under Secretary for the Colonies and serving on several committees looking into the state of English education. He became the Principal of Queens College, Birmingham in 1845 and the first president of the Birmingham and Midland Institute in 1853. His first wife, Mary, bore him eight sons and four daughters, leading some to suggest that he was trying to produce his own cricket

team. One of his sons, Edward, did indeed play cricket for England and became headmaster of Eton. Mary Lady Lyttelton died in 1850 and George Lord Lyttelton was married again in 1869 to Sybella Harriet, widow of Humphrey Francis Mildmay and daughter of George Clive. The marriage produced three daughters. George Lord Lyttelton was for many years subject to depressions and, in April 1876, he committed suicide by jumping from the landing of his London house. There is a window in memory of him in Halesowen Church. He was succeeded by his eldest son, Charles George Lyttelton.

12 *John Cavendish Lyttelton, 9th Viscount Cobham, who, as Lord Lieutenant of Worcestershire, handed over Halesowen's new Borough Charter to the Charter Mayor in 1936.*

Charles George 5th Lord Lyttelton and 8th Viscount Cobham (1842-1922)

Charles George Lyttelton was born in 1842 and educated at Eton and Trinity College, Cambridge. He was MP for East Worcestershire from 1868-74 and inherited the title of Lord Lyttelton from his father in 1876, followed by that of Viscount Cobham on the death of the last Duke of Buckingham in 1889. In 1878 he married Mary, daughter of Lord Chesham, who was descended from the Cavendishes of Chatsworth, but lived at Latimer in Buckinghamshire. This marriage brought the Lytteltons back into Whig political circles. Charles Lord Lyttelton became a governor of Halesowen Grammar School in 1878. Charles Viscount Cobham died in 1922.

John Cavendish Lyttelton 9th Viscount Cobham and 6th Lord Lyttelton (1881-1949)

John Cavendish Lyttelton inherited Hagley Hall in 1922. He was born in 1881 and served in the South African War and the Great War. He was MP for the Droitwich Division of Worcestershire from 1910-16. He married Violet Yolande, daughter of Charles Leonard, in 1908. He was a governor of Halesowen Grammar School from 1922 and rebuilt Hagley Hall after the fire of 1925. As Lord Lieutenant of Worcestershire, he handed over Halesowen's new Borough Charter to the Charter Mayor in 1936. He died in 1949.

Charles John Lyttelton 10th Viscount Cobham and 7th Lord Lyttelton (1909-77)

Charles John Lyttelton was born in 1909 and educated at Eton and Trinity College, Cambridge. He was Captain of the Worcester County Cricket team from 1936-9, and Vice-Captain of the M.C.C. on their tour of New Zealand in 1935-6. He served in the Second World War, marrying Elizabeth Alison, daughter of John Reeder Makeig-Jones, of Ottery St Mary, Devon, in 1942. He was Parliamentary candidate for Dudley and Stourbridge before succeeding his father in the Lords in 1949, and was Governor General of New Zealand from 1957 to 1961. He became Lord Lieutenant of Worcestershire in 1963 and died in 1977, succeeded by his son John William Leonard Lyttelton.

John Lyttelton 11th Viscount Cobham and 8th Lord Lyttelton

The present Viscount Cobham, John William Leonard Lyttelton, inherited Hagley Hall in 1977. He was born in 1943 and educated at Eton, Christ's College, New Zealand, and at the Royal Agricultural College, Cirencester. In 1974 he married Penelope Anne, daughter of Roy Cooper, but the marriage was dissolved in 1995. In 1997, he married Lisa Clayton, the former Birmingham accountant who was the first woman to sail single-handed and non-stop around the world.

The lord of the Manor Today

During the 18th and 19th centuries successive Lytteltons, as lords of the manor, sold the freeholds of most of their copyhold farms and business premises. This was often called enfranchisement, as a freeholder could vote in an election whereas a copyhold tenant could not. The manorial court therefore became less important as there were fewer transactions involving copyhold land and fewer tenants paying fines when they inherited or transferred property. Copyhold tenure was abolished under the Law of Property Act of 1922 and manorial courts became a thing of the past. The remaining copyholds were converted into ordinary leases, and the Lytteltons' agents concentrated on maximising the rents of the farms and premises held for a given number of years, and selling the right to work coal and other minerals under their land.

The title of lord of the manor now has little meaning, but as nominal owner of the soil, the lord of the manor was able to register his rights to any remaining common land under the Commons Registration Act of 1965. In some parishes, owners of manors have sold the courtesy title of lord of the manor to pretentious outsiders, but Lord Cobham remains lord of the manor of Halesowen. Lord Cobham also owns the advowson, or right to nominate the incumbent of St John's Church, Halesowen, but, in practice, this is done by the Bishop of Worcester.

Chapter II

IRONMASTERS AND NAILMAKERS

❧❧

Halesowen is on the south-west fringe of the Black Country, its built-up area even today following the limit of the workable coal seams. As early as 1307 the Abbot of Halesowen leased a coal mine at Coombs Wood for an annual rent of £4. The tenant, Henry Hill, was allowed to open two pits (*'duos puteos minere carbonis'*) and to employ four picks only in each mine (*'quattuor ligonibus in eadem minera'*).[1] The coal could have been used by local smiths in the working of iron, but the smelting of iron required the higher temperatures only attainable at that period by the burning of charcoal. The Abbot of Halesowen had ample woodland, particularly in Romsley and Hunnington, where coppiced trees could be cropped every nine or ten years to supply the charcoal burners.

13 *The New Hawne Colliery, c.1912. This mine was developed by the New British Iron Company, who purchased the mineral rights from the Attwood's trustees in 1864.*

Halesowen's abundant supply of coal was to prove crucial in the 18th century, when the technique of smelting iron in coke-fired furnaces was perfected. The coal measures extended south as far as a line roughly followed by the modern Halesowen bypass. Many ironmasters opened their own mines, such as the Attwoods of Hawne, owners of the Corngreaves Iron Works, who developed the Old Hawne Colliery. This mine was connected by a horse-drawn tramway to the Dudley Canal at Coombs Wood, where the wharf became known as Hawne Basin. Noah Hingley & Sons, owners of iron works at Netherton, opened up the Coombs Wood Colliery, after buying the mineral rights from Lord Lyttelton in 1893.

Iron Smelting

Up until the late medieval period, the process of iron-smelting involved placing iron ore between layers of charcoal in a small bowl-shaped pit. Air was introduced through a flue or forced in by foot-operated bellows. The furnaces were very small and could be constructed wherever iron ore could be mined and wood for charcoal cut down. These primitive furnaces did not produce sufficient heat to melt the metal, but did produce small crystals of iron which collected together to form a larger mass, or 'bloom', which could be removed from the furnace with iron tongues. The process created more waste than usable blooms. Nash, writing in around 1781, remarks that 'great quantities of iron cinders' had been found in the road leading from Causeway Green, in Warley Wigorn, towards Oldbury and near Langley. He conjectured that these waste materials from iron smelting could have dated from 'British, Roman, or Saxon times'.[2]

The blooms had to be reheated and hammered to remove impurities which would otherwise make the iron brittle. The earliest documentary evidence of such iron-working in Halesowen comes from the court rolls of 1312, when the Abbot of Hales gave permission to Richard Faber of Dudley, then living in Halesowen, 'to found and build a forge near the bank of Haymill, and to raise tin from which he may forge hatchets and other arms for the term of his life'.[3] This forge would probably have been located on the River Stour, with a water-wheel used to lift the forge hammer. The site may have been at the bottom of Mucklow Hill, where the place-name Haywood occurs, or at Hayseech, where the river forms the boundary with the parish of Rowley Regis. It could even have been at Oldbury, for a Halesowen Abbey rental of 1500 lists William Darby paying ten marks rent for a 'Blomesmythy' there.[4]

The Lyttelton family, who bought the Abbey in 1558, had 'bloomsmithies' at Cradley and Halesowen by 1566.[5] The 1601 inventory of goods of John Lyttelton of Frankley, lists amongst his possessions in Shropshire (Halesowen), goods 'in the smythes'. Here were 50 loads of charcoal valued at £16 13s. 4d., 40 wain-loads of iron stone worth £6 0s. 0d., and 'tooles and implementes for the same smythe' worth £3 6s. 8d.[6]

Hales Furnace

The location of John Lyttelton's 'smythes' is not clear, but soon after his death in 1601, the Lytteltons established a blast furnace at the foot of what became known as Furnace Hill, immediately north of the bridge carrying the old road from Halesowen to Dudley over the river Stour. Ironstone and charcoal could be loaded into the top of the furnace from the bridge. Damming the river to the east of the bridge enabled the installation of a water wheel, which opened and closed the huge wood and leather bellows and forced air into the furnace. At first the Lyttelton family ran Hales Furnace themselves. They had ample coppiced woodland to provide the charcoal, and brought iron ore to the site from a variety of sources. In 1609 John Lyttelton's widow, Meriel, made an agreement with Thomas Sutton alias Dudley to get ironstone from his estate at Russell Hall, near Dudley.[7]

The various iron works in the Stour valley must have been of great strategic importance during the Civil War. Both Sir Thomas Lyttelton, owner of Hales Furnace, and Lord Dudley, who owned Cradley Forge, were active Royalists. It is likely that by 1642 both of these sites had come under the control of the Stourbridge ironmaster, Richard Foley, who had a chain of furnaces and forges in the Stour valley. Prince Rupert stayed at Foley's house in Stourbridge in October 1642, probably anxious that his products should be supplied only to the Royalists. In February 1644 Thomas Leveson, Governor of the Royalist garrison at Dudley, was instructed 'to seize upon Foley of Stourbridge and cause him to send to Worcester 1,900 pike heads which is behind hand with the King. And he provide 2,000 more with all possible speed, for which he shall be paid as he delivers them at Worcester.'[8] In 1658, Foley's agent, Isaac Tonks, was purchasing large quantities of coppice wood from Sir Henry Lyttelton, which can only have been destined for Cradley Forge or Hales Furnace.[9] Thomas Foley renewed the lease on Cradley Forge in 1662[10] and his son Philip Foley renewed the lease on Hales Furnace in 1669.[11]

The Foley Papers, now preserved at Hereford Record Office, include a 1660 agreement with a dealer called John Tyrer for the purchase of 1,000 'cords' of wood from Hagley, Romsley and Lutley at a price of £350. The agreement stipulated that each cord, or stack, of wood should measure 8ft. x 4ft. x 4ft.[12] Foley's charcoal burners would work in the woods and could take turf to cover the piles of wood. Under these conditions, the cut wood burnt very slowly, removing the impurities with the minimum loss of combustible material. The resulting charcoal would be put in sacks of about two cwt. each, making a 'load' of about 16 cwt., worth about £1. Two loads of charcoal were needed to produce every ton of pig iron.

In 1669, Thomas Foley handed over the management of his iron works in the Stour Valley to his youngest son, Philip. Philip Foley made a detailed account of the stock and debts he inherited. These accounts show that Hales Furnace was managed by John Downing, who had probably succeeded his father in this position, for a payment of £10 as a pension to Adam Downing is entered. The rent paid to Sir Henry Lyttelton for the furnace was £40 per annum, plus '£29 lost by the mills this year', suggesting that the huge demand for water to power the furnace bellows was draining the mill ponds of the mills higher up the stream. The vast appetite of such furnaces for coppice wood is illustrated by an entry in the 1668 accounts of 1,010 loads of charcoal, supplied to Hales Furnace by Isaac Tonks, at a cost of £1,192.[13]

The Foley Papers also include a renewal of the lease of Hales Furnace from Sir Henry Lyttelton to Philip Foley for a further 11 years, starting from March 1669. The lease included all the implements and utensils at the furnace and also 'all that one cottage or dwelling house wherein John Downing now dwelleth situate nigh to the said Furnace'. The tenants of the corn mill and blade mill upstream of the furnace were obliged to let down sufficient water to power the furnace bellows. Philip Foley agreed to purchase up to 1,200 cords of coppice wood each year from Sir Henry Lyttelton's woods and Sir Henry Lyttelton agreed to supply timber to repair the bellows and stone from his own quarry to replace the furnace hearth.[14] Philip Foley also preserved a series of yield accounts of his works between 1667 and 1672 from which the production figures given in the table for Hales Furnace have been taken.[15]

Pig iron produced at Hales Furnace, 1667-72

Year	Tons
1667	357
1668	655
1669	575
1670	635
1671	444
1672	608

Most of the pig iron generated at Hales Furnace went to Thomas Foley's forges at West Bromwich, Wednesbury and Little Aston, where it was refined into bar iron. The bars were then cut into thin strips, suitable for making nails, at Foley's nearby Bustleholme Slitting Mill.

In November 1676, Philip Foley was negotiating the transfer of Hales Furnace, and the three forges and slitting mill at West Bromwich, to the Birmingham ironmaster Humphrey Jennens. According to the sale particulars he drew up, Hales Furnace was held on an 11-year lease, commencing 23 March 1669. The rent was £102 18s. per annum, but the mills were sub-let at £40 a year. Jennens would be obliged to buy wood from the landlord at 6s. per cord, and to keep the furnace in repair.[16] Philip Foley undertook to buy about half the product of the furnace, that is 300 tons per year, or six tons per week, at £5 5s. per ton. Humphrey Jennens must have accepted these terms, as he ran the works until the various leases on the premises ran out in 1691. By this date Philip Foley was in dispute with Jennens over his failure to repair Hales Furnace, and decided to take the premises back under his own control.

In 1692, Philip Foley formed a new partnership to run the Stour Valley ironworks. The cash holder was to be John Wheeler of Wollaston Hall (formerly the manager

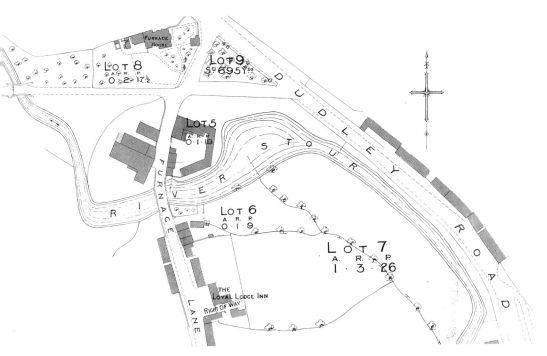

14 *The site of Hales Furnace from a sale catalogue of 1909.*

of Cradley Forge), who held a quarter of the shares. Richard Avenant of Shelsley Forge also had a quarter share. The other partners, who each held one sixth of the shares, were Philip Foley himself, then of Prestwood, Staffordshire, and Richard Wheeler and Paul Foley of Stoke Edith, Hereford.[17] They continued to employ John Downing as manager of Hales Furnace at a salary of £60 per year. Surviving accounts for 1692/3 show that only 210 tons of pig iron were cast at Hales Furnace that year. John and Zachary Downing leased Cradley Forge from Lord Ward in 1693 and may have agreed to take an assignment of the lease of Hales Furnace at about the same time. John Downing the younger of Furnace was buried at Halesowen in 1696, and another John Downing of Furnace was buried there in 1699. Zachary Downing continued to run Hales Furnace until 1703.

The Foley partnership negotiated a new lease of the furnace from Sir Charles Lyttelton in 1703.[18] There are production figures for Hales Furnace amongst the Foley papers for 1704/5 (683 tons) and 1705/6 (466 tons). Hales Furnace was then assigned to the Shropshire ironmaster Richard Knight, who entered the Foley partnership in 1707. Knight's stake in the partnership running the Stour Valley works increased as that of the Foleys decreased. He introduced other shareholders such as Sir Thomas Lyttelton and Clement Acton, who had succeeded Zachary Downing as the manager of Hales Furnace. Acton had four sons and two daughters baptised at Halesowen from 1704 onwards. By the time he made his will in 1726, Clement Acton was living in Kingswinford. He left to his wife Mary 'the

interest benefit and profit of six hundred pounds part of my stock in partnership at
Halesowen Furnace and Cookley and Whittington Forges, during her natural life,
in full of the provision intended for her by articles before intermarriage'. Clement
Acton's executors still held shares in the business in 1736. Halesowen Furnace was
then rented for £69 per year from Sir Thomas Lyttelton, who was also the major
shareholder in the Stour Valley works, with an investment of £4,500. Other major
shareholders were Richard, Edward and Ralph Knight and Joseph Cox, who each
had £2,500 invested.[19]

The Knight family preserved accounts of their various Stour Valley works from
which the following production figures are taken:

Pig iron produced at Hales Furnace, 1726-72

Year	Tons	Year	Tons
1726–27	477	1750–51	739
1727–28	525	1751–52	79
1728–30	712	1752–53	666
1730–31	724	1753–54	148
1731–32	630	1754–55	392
1732–33	514	1755–56	593
1733–34	490	1756–57	117
1734–35	649	1757–58	821
1735–36	347	1758–59	624
1736–37	321	1759–60	0
1737–38	609	1760–61	475
1738–39	699	1761–62	0
1739–40	177	1762–63	582
1740–41	780	1763–64	66
1741–42	570	1764–65	425
1742–43	753	1765–66	159
1743–44	632	1766–67	509
1744–45	758	1767–68	0
1745–46	0	1768–69	121
1746–47	575	1769–70	0
1747–48	0	1770–71	0
1748–49	517	1771–72	248
1749–50	0		

In 1742 Edward Knight of Cookley, ironmaster, renewed his lease of Hales Furnace
from Sir Thomas Lyttelton for a further 21 years, at an annual rent of £67 5s. The
property comprised the dwelling house inhabited by Clement Acton (probably the
son of the earlier manager) and the house where the stock taker lived. Equipment
listed in the lease included the furnace bellows, four coal rakes and one mine rake,
all with iron teeth, two bank shovels, one 'tweer nook', eight iron rings, four furnace
shovels, four iron hammers for breaking stone, one iron ringer hammer, two iron
slopping hooks, one 'iron quost', one 'skumming batt', two cynder hooks, one iron

15   The Loyal Lodge Inn, *Furnace Hill, 1973. The date stone IGM 1736 probably refers to a family called Grove. The inn was called the* Loyal Lodge *at the Furnace in 1822.*

stopper, one iron gage, one iron thruster, one iron loom bar, two iron plackets and one iron pig shovel. There was also a large wooden beam for weighing iron, two coal wheelbarrows and two stone wheelbarrows.[20]

Sir Thomas Lyttelton was to allow Edward Knight timber to repair the great bridge that stood in the highway leading to the furnace and was commonly called Furnace Bridge. If there was any shortage of water to power the bellows, Knight was able to demand that the tenant of Sir Thomas's corn mill above the furnace should immediately draw the floodgates or millgates to let down more water. Edward Knight was to take all the hearth stone required for the furnace from Sir Thomas's quarry at Hasbury and buy all his wood for charcoal from Sir Thomas's woods in the parishes of Halesowen, Frankley, Hagley, Arley and Rowley. Each load or cord of wood was to be eight feet in length, four feet in height and three feet in breadth, and to be purchased at the current market price. There are regular entries in Sir Thomas Lyttelton's account books of sales of wood to Edward Knight, such as the purchase of £376-worth of coalwood in 1747. The potential impact of this trade on the local landscape is illustrated by an entry in the same account book in 1719, when Isaac Brettell of Romsley was fined £50 for cutting several parcels of timber on his farm and doing damage to the Dales Wood.[21]

In 1757-8, Halesowen Furnace produced 821 tons of pig iron and made a profit of £1,024, but, by this time, charcoal-fired furnaces were beginning to be replaced with those designed to burn coke. In its last year of operation, 1771-2, it produced only 248 tons of pig iron. After its closure as a furnace, its water wheel was used to power a forge hammer. The Tithe Award of 1844 lists Furnace Forge as occupied by a spade and shovel maker called George Wood. In 1873, George William Lord Lyttelton sold Furnace Forge to the then tenant, Joseph Sidaway of Halesowen, spade and shovel manufacturer.[22] Joseph Sidaway lived at Furnace House, which stood to the north of the forge, close to the junction of Furnace Hill with Dudley Road. A Joseph Sidaway was still in business there in 1916 and the site is marked on the 1919 Ordnance Survey map as a spade and shovel works.

Cradley Forge

Pig iron from the furnace needed further refinement at the forge before it could be used in the various branches of the iron industry. In the forge, the pig iron was repeatedly heated on a charcoal hearth called a finery to sweat out impurities. It was then transferred to a coal-fired hearth called a chafery where it was hammered into conveniently sized bars. The forge therefore used waterpower not only for the bellows of the two hearths but also to lift the hammers. Edward Lord Dudley, owner of the manor of Rowley Regis, on the Staffordshire side of the Stour, built a blast furnace and forge at Cradley in 1603. Initially it was run by a manager, Humphrey Lowe, but in 1619 Lord Dudley's illegitimate son, Dud Dudley, was induced to leave his studies at Oxford in order to manage his father's works at Pensnett and Cradley. It was here that Dud Dudley claimed to have devised a method of making iron with coal, rather than with charcoal, which was thought at the time to be the only fuel able to burn at sufficiently high a temperature to make iron. Dudley's critics never accepted that he perfected the process of making iron with coal, an invention generally attributed to Abraham Darby of Coalbrookdale, nearly one hundred years later.

By 1636, Cradley Forge had been leased by Lord Dudley to Richard Foley of Stourbridge, who, according to equally dubious local tradition, was the first to introduce the slitting mill into this country. There is no doubt, however, that Foley's slitting mill at Hyde gave a significant boost to the local nail industry, and that he was the first to build a network of furnaces, forges and slitting mills in the district. Foley's manager at Cradley was John Wheeler, who appears in Halesowen parish registers as John Wheeler 'of ye Forge' in 1658.

Cradley Forge must have been extremely busy during the Civil War when Richard Foley was supplying huge amounts of weaponry to the Royalists. When Edward, Lord Dudley died without a legitimate heir in 1643, his son-in-law, Humble Ward, the son of a London goldsmith, inherited his iron works. Charles I wasted no time in recruiting Ward to the cause, knighting him in 1643 and creating him Lord Ward in 1644. Lord Ward's estates were sequestered by Parliament in 1651 but discharged in 1656. Lord Ward died in 1670 and was succeeded by his son Edward. When Edward, Lord Ward's mother died in 1697, he was created Lord Dudley and Ward.

In 1662, Lord Ward leased Cradley Furnace and Forge to Richard Foley's son, Thomas Foley of Great Whitley.[23] He in turn passed control to his son Philip in 1669, and it is Philip Foley's surviving accounts which give the production figures shown opposite.

In 1674, Philip Foley prepared an account of his Stour Valley works in order that he could assign the lease to Sir Clement Clerk and John Foorth. He described

Bar iron produced at Cradley Forge, 1668-1673

Year	Tons
1668	107
1669	62
1670	90
1671	90
1672	96
1673	86

Cradley Forge as capable of producing 100 tons of bar iron per year. It was leased from Lord Ward at £80 per annum, but the nearby corn mills were sub-let for £40. The lessee also had the right to get ironstone at Amblecote and to buy wood for charcoal from Lord Ward at 7s. a cord. Although the transfer to Clerk and Foorth went ahead, the partners fell out and by 1681 the Stour Valley works, including Cradley Forge, were under the control of a new partnership of former Foley managers: John Wheeler, formerly of Cradley Forge, Richard Avenant of Shelsley Forge and John Downing of Hales Furnace.

In 1693, Lord Ward leased Cradley Forge to John and Zachary Downing of Halesowen. Again they were given liberty to dig ironstone 'upon the waste ground called Amblecoat or the enclosures there made' to the extent of 'one thousand loads or blooms of ironstone yearly'.[24] In 1697, Zachary Downing leased Lye Mill from John Addenbrooke and converted it into another forge. By 1710, however, Zachary Downing was bankrupt and Lye and Cradley Forges were sold to the executors of John Wheeler. In 1724, Richard and Edward Wheeler sold the business to Edward Kendall of Stourbridge. The conveyance includes an inventory of stock remaining at Cradley Furnace, Cradley Forge, Cradley Rodmill and Lye Forge. In 1774 Lord Dudley leased Cradley Forge and Cradley Furnace in Rowley and Cradley, together with Cradley Slitting Mills or New Mills and pools and workmen's houses, to the ironmasters Richard Croft of Stourbridge and William Croft of Wombourne for 20 years, at a rent of £210 per annum. The tenant was able to take limestone from Lord Dudley's estate at Coneygre and Old Park and to purchase timber from Lord Dudley's woods for converting into 'cole wood'.[25] The charcoal furnace at Cradley may have continued in operation longer than its rivals, for Samuel Evers & Sons, who took over the site in 1826, were still advertising that their horsenail rods were made from charcoal iron as late as 1860. The site was later taken over by Jones and Lloyd, who continued to make anchors and chains at Cradley Forge until the 1930s.

Halesowen Forge

Successive leases of Hales Furnace contain clauses ensuring that the millers upstream let down enough water to operate the furnace bellows. In 1670 John Downing, the manager of Hales Furnace, ensured a good supply of water by leasing the mills himself.[26] These included a malt mill just below Halesowen's principal corn mill at

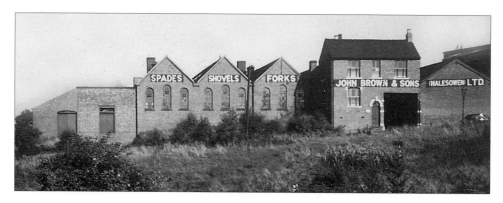

16   *The premises of John Brown & Son, Forge Lane, c.1950.*

the bottom of Mucklow Hill. The malt mill was turned into a forge, perhaps when the corn mill became a slitting mill prior to 1762. Both sites were leased by Lord Lyttelton to William Ward in 1788.[27] A further 21-year lease of the slitting mill and forge was made to Messrs Grazebrook and Whitehouse, iron and coalmasters, in 1809.[28] The forge seems to have become a separate business again when the slitting mill was converted to a gun barrel works by Messrs Rose. By 1844 the forge, shops, yard and pool were sub-let to William Wood, a spade and shovel maker. By 1855 he had been succeeded by Joseph Hipkiss, a vice and anvil maker. A plan of the premises in 1873 shows Halesowen Forge with the pool, buildings, warehouse and tenement, leased by Hipkiss Brothers from the gun barrel manufacturers, Rose Brothers.[29] From about 1900 until the 1960s, John Brown & Sons manufactured spades, shovels and forks at Halesowen Forge.

Halesowen Slitting Mill

Before the iron produced by the furnaces and forges of the Stour valley could be used by the nailers, the bars had to be reheated and laboriously cut into square rods using chisels. This process was revolutionised by the slitting mill, first introduced into this area by Richard Foley, who built his slitting mill at Hyde Mill, near Kinver, in 1628. Halesowen's principal corn mill was converted into a slitting mill in the mid-18th century. It was situated at the bottom of Mucklow Hill, just south of the bridge carrying the road from Birmingham into the town. There is no evidence that it was converted into a slitting mill by the Foley partnership, which ran Hales Furnace until 1705, or by Richard Knight, who took over in that year. Indeed the corn mill was still functioning in 1742, for Edward Knight took out a new lease on the furnace and corn mill in that year.[30]

The corn mill had definitely become a slitting mill by 1762, when it is mentioned by the poet William Shenstone, of the Leasowes. Writing to his friend, the Rev. Richard Graves, he refers to a cascade in his garden which 'proceeds a few hundred

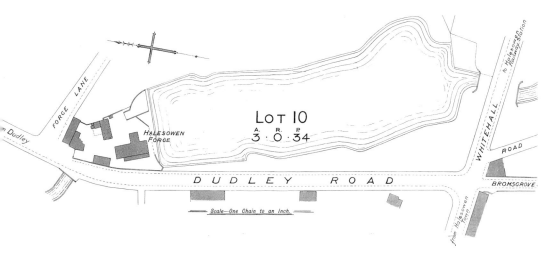

17 *Site of Halesowen Forge, 1909.*

yards, where it rolls and slits iron for manufactures of all kinds.'[31] There were two mill ponds for the slitting mill, one extending back along the Stour towards Manor Abbey and the other forming a lake within the grounds of the Leasowes. It was this latter pond which was cut in two by the construction of the Dudley Canal in 1798. A Lyttelton rental of 1808 records the rent paid by Mathias Attwood for the land belonging to the Leasowes on one side of the embankment, and a separate rent for 'Mr Ward's land parted by the Canal'. Mr Ward held the slitting mill on a 21-year lease commencing in 1788, at £165 a year.[32] The lease was not renewed, probably because there was then a much more efficient process for drawing out iron for nail making.

In 1809 Lord Lyttelton leased the slitting mill and forge to Messrs Grazebrook and Whitehouse, coal and ironmasters, for 21 years.[33] This partnership included Thomas Worrall Grazebrook, of Stourton Castle, Kinver, Michael Grazebrook, of Audnam Bank, Kingswinford, and Benjamin Whitehouse, of Netherton. Michael Grazebrook leased nearby Belle Vue House from the Male family in the 1830s. A contributor to the *Halesowen Who's Who* in 1951 described an 1813 date-stone in the gable end of the mill and claimed that the water-wheel was one of the largest in the country. There is a long correspondence between Lord Lyttelton and his agent, commencing in 1817, about the spiralling costs of repairs to the mill, particularly the provision of timber fit for use by a millwright. Lord Lyttelton explains his reluctance to press for the £340 annual rent as being due to 'the bad state of the iron trade and the unsettled claim of wood to repair, they having spent large sums on their premises and their high rent under adverse circumstances'. The tenants also wanted to erect a new house at nearby Birch Hill. Messrs Grazebrook and Whitehouse evidently did not renew their lease, for the mill was soon turned over to the manufacture of gun barrels.

18   *Halesowen Steel Co., 1973. This was the site of Halesowen's ancient corn mill. It was subsequently a slitting mill, a gun-barrel boring mill, and latterly, a tube and steel works.*

Nail Making

The process of nail manufacture was carried out by thousands of independent nailers in all the towns and villages within reasonable distance of the slitting mills, at hearths attached to their cottages. They obtained their rod iron from men like Humphrey Hill of Cradley, who is mentioned in the 1625 Quarter Sessions as 'a driver into the country with nails'. Many such wholesalers were farmers, or even minor gentry. George Harris, one of the wealthiest men in Hunnington, described himself as a 'nailer' in his will of 1633. Phillip Boddiley of Halesowen in the County of Salop gave his occupation as 'nailer' in his will of 1656. Robert Brettell, a well-to-do Romsley farmer, also called himself a 'nailer' in his will of 1682, which divided his shop tools and bellows equally between his sons William and Robert. The friends and neighbours who compiled the inventory of the ironmonger Robert Bloomer of Cradley in 1683, put down a nominal sum of £100 for 'all nails and debts owed to Mr Robert Bloomer in the country where he traded'. The wealthiest nail ironmonger was surely William Jeston of Cradley, who also died in 1683, owed £1,244 4s. 8d. 'as appears by his debt book and iron ware at home and abroad in nayles and other iron goods'. The nailers brought their finished nails to the wholesaler's warehouse, where they invariably complained that the scales used were inaccurate and that they were underpaid.

19 *Webb's Green Farm, Lapal, home of the Bissell family, Halesowen's leading nail ironmongers in the 18th and 19th centuries.*

In the 18th and 19th centuries, the wholesalers became fewer and more opulent, tending to call themselves nail ironmongers. A good example was Thomas Bissell, who leased Webb's Green Farm from the lord of the manor, Sir Thomas Lyttelton, in 1722.[34] The Bissells made several advantageous marriages. Thomas Bissell married Elizabeth Smith in 1786, bringing Horsepool Farm, Hunnington, into the family estate. In 1814, Thomas John Smith Bissell married Charlotte Powell, co-heiress of Samuel Powell of Halesowen, who owned extensive property in the town, including several houses in Great Cornbow. Soon after the Dudley Canal was opened in 1797, Thomas Bissell built a new nail warehouse beside the bridge carrying Manor Lane over the canal. The Bissells owned a malting and grocer's shop on the High Street opposite the *Old Lyttelton Arms*. They were probably amongst the group of nail masters who paid their out-workers partly in expensive provisions, contrary to the Truck Acts. The family ceased business in about 1870.

Another example of a wealthy nail ironmonger was Thomas Green of Greenhill Farm, Mucklow Hill, who died in 1753. His son Edward Green built a new nail warehouse on land at Greenhill leased from Lord Lyttelton in 1774. Edward Green died in 1794, leaving money in trust for the poor of Halesowen. His unusual castellated house still stands at the top of Mucklow Hill. Edward Green's business was taken over by Joseph Darby, whose widowed daughter, Amelia Wheeler, started a girls' school at Greenhill House in 1849. Joseph Darby built another new nail warehouse in 1828; it was near the canal at Haywood, and was linked to Mucklow Hill by a private road. This was the same site on which Walter Somers later built Haywood Forge.[35]

One of the most respectable nail ironmongers in the town was John Green, who married Elizabeth, daughter of Walter Woodcock, in 1784. They rented the large house with railings formerly numbered 24, Hagley Street, from Elizabeth's brother, also Walter Woodcock, who lived at Dovehouse Fields Farm, Hunnington

20   *Greenhill House, Mucklow Hill, 1974. The house was built by Edward Green, nail ironmonger, in about 1780. It was later a girls' boarding school run first by Amelia Wheeler, and later by Emmeline Harcourt.*

until his death in 1821. The business was continued by John and Elizabeth's son, John Green, who appears in early trade directories as a nail ironmonger, but in later years is listed only in the private residents' section as 'Green, John Esq. J.P., Hagley Street'. John Green bought the house from Walter Woodcock's executors in 1827,[36] and lived there until his death in 1869. His house stood next to Lloyd's Bank and was later occupied by the grocer, Charles Peach.

One of the best-known firms of nail ironmongers was Guest & Co., who took over the fine half-timbered house numbered 20, Great Cornbow, in about 1865. The partners in this firm were John George Reay of Dudley and Ephraim Ball, who later lived at the three-storey Georgian house next door called Cornbow House. They specialised in the manufacture of horse nails and horseshoes and, by

21   *Great Cornbow Works, partially demolished, 1958. Ephraim Ball's original nail warehouse was behind the half-timbered house numbered 20 Great Cornbow. He later lived at number 19, the three-storey Georgian house.*

1889, had 50 employees working there. They greatly extended the buildings and erected the tallest chimney in Halesowen. Ephraim Ball died in 1884, but the firm continued into the 1940s and sold their premises to Halesowen Borough Council for the building of the swimming pool. The half-timbered house was demolished in 1963.[37]

The Parliamentary Report on the Sweating System in 1889 suggested that 550 people in Halesowen were still employed in the manufacture of nails. These comprised 200 men and 350 women and boys. Two thirds of them worked in domestic nail shops, with equipment which had hardly changed since 1800. The remainder worked for one of the 20 nail factories in the town. The only surviving nail warehouse in Halesowen is on the corner of Laurel Lane and Powell Street, and belonged in 1901 to James Heague, iron, nail and chain manufacturer.

22 *James Heague's nail warehouse, Laurel Lane, 1973.*

Chain Making

With the introduction of machine-made nails in the 1830s, many nail makers adapted their hearths to make chain instead. The cast-iron rods used for nails could just as easily be hammered under heat into the oval shape required for chain links, the welded joint made when one link was joined to another proving as strong as any point in the casting. Much of the work was done by outworkers, both male and female, on hearths in small outhouses behind their cottages. Later firms specialising in particular types of chain brought the workers into larger factories, especially after the adoption of electric welding in the early 1900s. Chain making was largely confined to the growing industrial villages of Cradley, Cradley Heath, Netherton, Quarry Bank and Old Hill. Products ranged from small chain for blocks and tackle to anchor cables for ocean liners. The huge anchor chain for the Titanic was made by the firm of Noah Hingley & Son of Netherton in 1911. Each link was made

23 *Jones & Lloyd's Scotia Works, Colley Lane, Cradley, 1973.*

out of cast iron rod 3¼ ins. in diameter. Clifford Willetts, Mayor of Halesowen in 1950, was a chain maker at Henry Reece & Co., Cradley. The last firm in Cradley to make chains was Messrs Jones & Lloyd, who had works at Colley Lane and at Cradley Forge. The firm closed down around 1970.

Scythe Making

Another branch of the iron trade was that of making scythes. As early as 1346, the Abbot of Hales granted to Hugo le Cotiler 'a piece of land with a water course to make a certain workshop to grind knives, hatchets and other things which pertain to the smith's craft'.[38] In 1547 Henry Melley of Romsley paid 2s. 6d. rent for 'Smythes Tenement', leased to him by John Dudley, Earl of Warwick, along with a water mill, the 'Smethyfield' and a parcel of waste containing three acres.[39] He was probably an ancestor of John Melley of Farley, in the hamlet of Romsley, who described himself as a scythe maker in his will of 1605. He may have lived at what we now call Farley Cottage and used nearby Sling Pool to power his hammer and grind-stones. He left his biggest anvil in the 'over shop' to his son John, a smaller anvil to his son William, and his other tools to be divided between them. The trade was also carried on in the borough of Halesowen. A lease of Hales Furnace in 1669 mentions a blade mill, upstream of the furnace, powered by Cornbow Pool. In 1670 William Haughton was the occupant of the blade mill at Cornbow,[40] which was still in operation in 1742, when it is mentioned again in a lease of Hales Furnace.

Gun Barrels and Tubing

During the 18th century, several corn mills on the river Stour were converted to forges or gun-barrel boring mills. The gun barrels were made at the forge from strips of iron whose sides were bent over and welded longways to form the barrel.

24 *Brooklands, Great Cornbow, c.1910. The remains of Cornbow Mill can be seen on the extreme right of the house.*

25 *The restoration of Lutley Mill, 1974.*

The inside of the barrel was then drilled perfectly straight and the rifling introduced to spin the bullet in flight. The old corn mills were converted by millwrights like John Burr of Bundle Hill House, Halesowen, who was involved with Lutley Mill and, especially, Hayseech Mill, which had become a gun-barrel boring mill by 1795. A date-stone, 'Burr 1801', survives on one of the buildings at Hayseech. John Burr died in 1805, but his son John Burr (d.1856) and his grandsons Alfred (d.1875) and Arthur (d.1892) Burr continued to manufacture gun barrels at Hayseech into the 1860s. The mill was later taken over by the Birmingham Gun Barrel Company.[41] In the 1980s, it was converted into small industrial units by Eric Charles Emery.

By 1841, Halesowen Slitting Mill had become a gun-barrel manufactory, run by a partnership that included Thomas Edge, who lived near the mill at Birch Hill, and Aaron Rose, the owner of the *Plume of Feathers Inn*, Church Street. Thomas Edge died in 1848 and the business was carried on by the Rose family, who built a large house called the Mount standing high above Bromsgrove Street, opposite the works. The Rose brothers bought the freehold of the factory from Lord Lyttelton in 1881.[42] By 1875, the manufacture of tubing for the gas and water industries had become more profitable than guns, so the Rose family began to roll longer barrels for use as tubes. The manufacture of gun barrels was entirely given up about 1895. The family business was turned into a limited company known as the Halesowen Tube Company, which built a new factory on the corner of Prospect Road and Mucklow Hill, and was later known as the National Tube Company. The firm adopted the new technology of the weldless tube. This involved heating a solid cylindrical piece of steel so that a hole could be punched into one end. The resulting bottle shape was then rolled out so that the outside was lengthened and the hole preserved. The solid end was then cut off to make a tube. The former slitting mill site at the bottom of Mucklow Hill was gradually taken over by the Halesowen Steel Co. Ltd. This related company, founded in 1908, produced bright drawn steel, used in the production of motor cars, aircraft, ships and all engineering and electrical equipment. The process

26   *National Tube Company, Mucklow Hill, c.1950.*

involved pulling steel bars through a hard steel dye of a diameter smaller than the bars being drawn, producing bars of very accurate size with a bright smooth surface. The bars were then coated with a rust preventative and dispatched in wooden cases to the customers. During the Second World War, over 30,000 tons per year of bright drawn steel bars were produced by Halesowen Steel Company.

The largest factory making steel tubes was founded by Abraham Barnsley, who bought a site on the east side of the Dudley Canal at Coombs Wood from Lord Lyttelton in 1860. He manufactured tubes for gas, water, steam and bedstead purposes. The Barnsleys sold the works to Noah Hingley and Sons, who sold it on to Henry Howard. In partnership with Lloyd & Lloyd of Birmingham, Henry Howard bought more land, extended the works, and began to specialise in the lap welding of larger tubes, which were then welded end to end and coiled into

27   *Coombs Wood Works, 1863.*

extremely long lengths of tubing. In 1903, Lloyd & Lloyd amalgamated with A. & J. Stewart & Mendzies of Glasgow to form Stewarts & Lloyds Ltd. The works were now extended on to the west side of the canal, eventually covering an area of 56 acres, 23 of which were covered by iron roofs. From 1930 the company was able to use the new method of producing seamless steel tubes. During the Second World War, part of the works was given over to shell forging, with a total of 7,400,000 forgings being produced by 1945. In 1942 the firm got the contract for the design and installation of P.L.U.T.O., the Pipe Line Under The Ocean project. At its peak, Stewarts & Lloyds employed over 3,000 people on the site. Stewarts & Lloyds later became part of British Steel. When the works closed in 1990 British Steel, now known as Corus Plc, developed the site as the Coombs Wood Business Park.

Walter Somers Ltd

During the 19th century, many entrepreneurs were entering the local iron trade, casting, drop-forging, stamping and pressing iron products. Walter Somers had learnt his trade making railway axles and wheels at Derby, and came to the area as forge manager at Hill & Smith of Brierley Hill. In 1866, Walter Somers was ready to set up on his own and leased a small iron works beside the canal on the north side of Mucklow Hill.[43] It had a 40 h.p. steam engine, two coal-fired

28 *Walter Somers*
Ltd offices, Prospect
Road, c.1920.

furnaces, a 30cwt. steam hammer, and two swivelling wooden jib cranes to swing
the forgings from the furnace to the hammer. Walter Somers specialised in the
manufacture of heavy forgings such as crankshafts for steam engines and propeller
shafts for ships. Any profits he made were invested in new plant, and in 1884
he installed a four-ton steam hammer, to be followed in 1887 by a seven-ton
Nasmyth hammer. Soon a 12-ton hammer costing £1,000 was installed, but
even this was not enough. By forming a limited company, Walter Somers Ltd,

29   *Walter Somers Ltd. from the former Railway Station, 1973.*

in 1897, Somers was able to bring in sufficient funds to install a hydraulic press, able to exert a force of 600 tons. In 1905 he bought an even bigger 3,600-ton steam hydraulic press at a cost of £8,500. The works had to be enlarged to accommodate the huge machine, and Somers's 'ommer' could be heard a mile away, often working throughout the night.

After the death of Walter Somers in 1917, his son Seth Somers became chairman; his brothers William and Frank were also directors. Seth Somers had bought the Grange, the former home of the Lea Smith family. He started the Somers' Sports and Social Club in the house in 1951, and also founded the Seth Somers Trust, which still owns Halesowen Cricket Ground. Now known as Somers Forge Ltd, the factory on Mucklow Hill is still a prominent local landmark, and the present 4,000-ton press makes it a forge with one of the largest capacities in the country.

Tanneries

Even before Halesowen received a market charter in 1220, there must have been butchers buying livestock on market day and selling the hides on to local tanners. There are several transactions recorded in the court rolls of the 1340s where Milo the Tanner is accumulating land in the common fields of Hasbury. The tannery at Cornbow dates back at least to the 16th century when it was run by Richard Wight, whose son Roger married Margery Hawkes in 1561. In 1614 William Wight gave 20s. a year to the poor of Halesowen, charged on the Bank House in Great Cornbow. When he died in 1628 he had leather and bark in his tanhouse and three green hides worth £13 13s. 4d., plus leather and hides at his house valued at £9 10s. 0d. In 1652, John and William Wight, both described as tanners, were jurors at an inquiry into Halesowen charities. After the inquisition, the tan pits seem to have passed into the possession of Halesowen Free School. In 1657, the tanner John Wight, of 'Porchhouse' was buried at Halesowen. Subsequent references to tanners in the town include Robert Bell in 1697, and Thomas Sansom, whose children by his wife Ann née Bradley were baptised at the parish church from 1747 onwards. Thomas Sansom died in 1762 and his business was continued by John Bradley of

30 *The tannery cottages which stood on Tanhouse Lane, near Cornbow Bridge, c.1900.*

31   *'Denstone', the Gas Works manager's house, next to the* Vine Inn, *1963.*

Cornbow House. The scale of the tannery business can be judged by the 1810 agreement whereby John Bradley paid £550 for the bark to be peeled off the fall of trees on Lord Lyttelton's estates that year.[44] John Bradley died in 1814 leaving the tannery to his son James. An 1820 deed, appointing new trustees for the Grammar School, includes 'all that messuage or tenement, nail shop, garden and premises situate in Little Cornbow Street, in the borough of Halesowen aforesaid, now in the occupation of James Bradley; also all that bark mill, barn and tan-yard, situate in the Borough of Halesowen aforesaid, now in the possession of the said James Bradley'.[45] James Bradley died in 1829, aged 57 years. Thomas Compson then took over the business. In 1839 he owned the tannery tenement and the currying shop, and leased the remaining part of the works from the trustees of the Grammar School. Thomas Compson employed five men at the tannery in 1851; he ran the business until his death in 1872, when the tannery was incorporated into the nearby gasworks. The tannery cottages were demolished before 1932 when Frank Somers included a picture of them in his book *Halas, Hales, Halesowen.*

Gas Works

At a meeting on 29 April 1836 chaired by the Halesowen solicitor, William Steel Hayes, it was resolved to establish the Halesowen Gas Light Company.[46] A site was

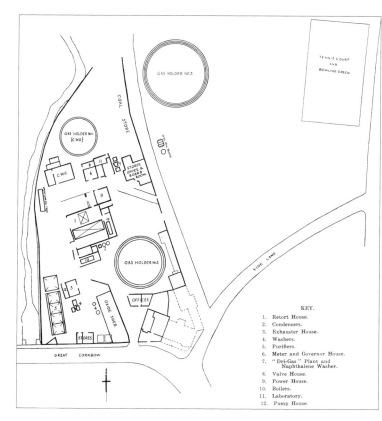

32 *Plan of Halesowen Gas Works, 1935.*

KEY.

1. Retort House.
2. Condensers.
3. Exhauster House.
4. Washers.
5. Purifiers.
6. Meter and Governor House.
7. "Dri-Gas" Plant and Naphthalene Washer.
8. Valve House.
9. Power House.
10. Boilers.
11. Laboratory.
12. Pump House.

found on part of the old tannery, adjacent to Cornbow Bridge, and the shareholders accepted the £770 tender of John Hobbins, gas engineer, to erect the plant. In the event, the works were completed by August 1837 at a cost of £1,148. The first manager, Thomas Siviter, was required to lay the mains, find coal and lime, regulate the burners, pay his workers' wages, and collect all rents, cash and income: all for a salary of £75 per year. It was as well that he had further sources of income, running the *Pool Inn* (subsequently called the *Cock*, and later the *Vine Inn*) and also manufacturing gas tubes at a factory at Rumbow. His son Charles Siviter carried on the tube works at Rumbow, where another son, James, ran the *Plough and Harrow*

33 *Gas holder No. 3, Tanhouse Lane, 1963.*

Inn. The streets of Halesowen were first lit by gas in 1840, the cost of £2 2s. per lamp per year being charged to the Surveyors of Highways.

In 1864 the then shareholders—Edward Moore, surgeon of Townsend House, Thomas Bissell, nail manufacturer of Greenfields, Charles Bloxham, surgeon of Great Cornbow, Richard Trewolla, draper of Great Cornbow and Thomas Siviter, gas tube manufacturer of Rumbow—sold their shares to the newly formed Halesowen Gas Company Ltd for £2,050. In 1865 the Gas Works site was extended by taking over the remainder of the old tannery and erecting a second gas holder. The Tan House was converted into offices, including a board room and stores. By the Halesowen Gas Act of 1883, the company became a statutory undertaking. A Board of Trade Order gave the Company extra powers in 1924, enabling a further extension of the site and the building of a 400,000 cubic feet capacity gas holder to the east of Tan House Lane. By 1935 Halesowen Gas Company had 5,060 customers consuming 99,694,000 cubic metres of gas per year.

The Halesowen Gas Company was taken over by West Midlands Gas Board in 1949. As it was a small works with no possibility of further expansion, gas production on the site was phased out and the town coupled to the production grid. Most of the gas used came from Dudley, but on occasion supplies were derived from as far away as Walsall. The last Gas Works manager was John H. Wainwright, who lived at the elegant Edwardian manager's house named 'Denstone', next to the *Vine Inn*. The Gas Works site was purchased from West Midlands Gas Board by Halesowen Borough Council in 1963, and the remaining buildings and plant were demolished in 1964.

Button Making

Another by-product of a cattle market is animal horns, which were used, amongst other things, for the manufacture of horn buttons. The editor of *Pigot's Directory* of 1822 observed that Halesowen was 'chiefly noted for its manufactory of nails; but there is a very extensive manufactory of pearl and horn buttons'. The directory listed Joseph Harris, pearl and horn button maker as living in the High Street. Harris's father, an earlier Joseph Harris, kept the *Plume of Feathers Inn* on Church Street, now occupied by the three shops called Church Street Chambers. In his will of 1803, the elder Harris mentioned two sums of £100 which he had loaned Joseph Harris and his partner George Hinchliffe in order to set up a button manufactory. The original premises were on the south side of Peckingham Street and backed onto the Congregational Church, of which Joseph Harris was a founder member.[47] The enterprise flourished and moved to larger premises on the west side of Birmingham Street. Joseph Harris lived in the old house in High Street, more recently occupied by Peplow's the jeweller; he died in 1844. His son William Harris was a printer and stationer in the premises later occupied by Major Hackett, the grocer. Joseph Harris's partner, the solicitor George Hinchliffe, built Comberton House, which still stands in Great Cornbow, where the brickwork either side of the door is inscribed with the initials GH and the date 1818.

34 *James Grove's Button Factory, Stourbridge Road, 1973.*

About 1838, Joseph Harris passed the management of the button manufactory to his son Thomas Harris, who built a much larger factory at Spring Hill, on the steep bank above Hagley Road. It was approached by a private road now known as The Drive, and comprised a warehouse, stabling, pressing shops and more than three acres of land. Thomas Harris lived next to the works in a house called Spring Villa. The gardens of this house included lawns, shrubberies, a large pond and a boathouse, all laid out in a style to rival Miss Attwood's grounds at the Leasowes.

By 1850 Thomas Harris had moved to Bartley Green, leaving his son William Joseph Harris to run the Spring Hill factory. In fact it was a former apprentice, James Grove, who proved to be the more able manager of the concern. He operated the factory until 1857, when he left to set up his own button factory in Birmingham Street. Another apprentice, Thomas Coley, also set up his own button works on Highfield Lane. As Thomas Coley & Son, the firm continued at Highfield Works until about 1885. The Rev. Henry Fisher, curate of Halesowen, gave evidence on button making to the Children's Employment Commission in 1863. He stated that there were then 'three button factories employing together about 150 persons, principally women or girls'.[48] Button manufacture at Spring Hill was continued by William Joseph Harris until about 1880. A descendant of the Harris family, Leslie George Harris, was later to establish the famous Harris Brush Works at Stoke Prior. The Spring Hill factory was later used by Samuel Williams' Perambulator & Manufacturing Co. Ltd, which made mail carts and children's tricycles as well as prams. The factory has only recently been demolished.

James Grove opened his first button factory in 1857, at premises on the corner of Birmingham Street and Cornbow, rented from his father-in-law William Henry Rose, a spade and shovel maker.[49] The business prospered and in 1866, at the sale of the Attwood estate, he was able to buy a large plot of land on Stourbridge Road; the Bloomfield Works opened in 1867 and soon outstripped the production of the Harris button works at Spring Hill. In 1882, James Grove took into partnership his two older sons, George Frederick Grove, of Church View, and Arthur James Grove of Bloomfield House. A third son, Ernest Harry Grove, practised as a solicitor in Halesowen and was clerk to the Halesowen Rural District Council. He founded the firm of E.H. Grove & Son, of Church Steps House, at the top of the High Street. James Grove himself lived at The Cedars, Stourbridge Road, until his death in 1886. James Grove & Sons Ltd is still in production, although only a small proportion of their products is now made from animal horns.

Chapter III

SHOPS AND SHOPKEEPERS

Given the huge economic potential of Halesowen and its hamlets, it is highly likely that a regular, if unofficial, market was held in the town prior to Henry III's grant of the manor of Halesowen to the Bishop of Winchester in 1215. When the Bishop fulfilled his part of the bargain and established an abbey at Halesowen, it was natural that the newly appointed Abbot should attempt to maximise its income by obtaining a market charter and re-planning the town on the lines of a borough. The fashion of the time dictated that a borough should have a market-place, a market hall and building plots (or 'burgages') where merchants (or 'burgesses') might establish new businesses.

In 1220, the Abbot of Hales obtained from Henry III licence to hold a market every week on Wednesdays and a fair lasting two days at the Feast of St Denis (9 October). Three years later, the date of the fair was changed to the feast of St Kenelm (17 July). This change was designed to exploit the pilgrims who travelled through Halesowen to the place on the boundary of Romsley and Clent where the obscure but saintly Mercian Prince Kenelm had reputedly been murdered. In 1344, the Abbot of Hales obtained a new market charter from the Crown, changing the market day to Monday and establishing a four-day fair at the Feast of St Barnabas (11 June).

The rules of trading at Halesowen market were settled in the court of the borough. As the sale of cattle was the most important aspect of trade in a market town, it is not surprising that many of the decisions of the court concerned the misdemeanors of local butchers. In 1473 the court ordered that all Halesowen butchers were 'to have all and every hide and little hide of cattle slaughtered by them for selling lying in the windows of their shops during the whole time that they may have any meat of the said cattle for selling'.[1] In 1489, the court again ordered that 'no butchers should put the garbage or blood of any beasts in any road within the borough under penalty of 1s. each'.[2] In 1493 John Smith of Lapal was said to have 'killed his beasts for selling in the market, outside the town, against the ordinance thus made'. He was fined 6s. 8d.[3] John Smith was accused of overloading the commons of Ridgacre in 1494,[4] and in 1500, John Smith, butcher, was fined 4d. for overstocking the common pasture at Illey.[5]

The Halesowen Churchwardens' Accounts contain tantalising references to the re-planning of the centre of the town in 1539.[6] A sum of £3 12s. 2d. was paid 'towards the making of the new street and the market house'. Edward Nicholas and his son were paid 12d. for two days' work, a sum of 9s. was paid for tiling the house, William Green was paid 2s. 6d. for laths and Mr Taylor, John Hidley and Thomas Smith all loaned money for the project. In 1541 there is a further payment of 6s. 8d. to Sir John 'of money he laid down for paving of the new street'. The date is significant because Halesowen Abbey had recently been sold to Sir John Dudley. Those buildings not needed for its conversion into the home farm of the manor were being demolished, and the building materials were available for re-use. The market house is referred to by William Harris in his 1831 history of Halesowen. He describes it as a 'spacious building, with a large and commodious room over it for public business; a prison was attached to it'. By 1800 it was in such poor repair that Lord Lyttelton offered it to the inhabitants at a peppercorn rent if they would maintain it. The offer was not taken up and the building was demolished. The 'new street' may have been the Bull Ring or, more likely, the street sometimes called Cross Square, which connected Great Cornbow and Little Cornbow, where the old market cross stood until 1907. The market house probably occupied the site used for the county police station in 1847.

In 1608, the lord of the manor, Meriel Lyttelton, caused a proclamation to be read in the neighbouring market towns, that the borough of Halesowen 'have had for a long time, a small meeting on the Sabbath day, for the buying and selling of butter, cheese and fruit' which was contrary to the word of God, His Majesty's laws and displeasing to Mrs Lyttelton. The proclamation recited the ancient grant to the town of a weekly market on Monday and a fair on St Barnabas Day (11 June), and urged His Majesty's loving subjects to make use of this market and fair to dispose of their commodities.[7]

During the Civil War and the Commonwealth the small copper coins formerly produced under monopolies granted by James I and Charles I grew very scarce. Although it was illegal to manufacture such coins, many local tradesmen chose to have penny, halfpenny and farthing coins produced to fill the gap and to promote trade. These coins usually had the date, the tradesman's name or initials and often a representation of his trade, such as candles for a tallow chandler, or a malt shovel for a maltster. Only two such trade tokens are known for Halesowen, those of William Bodely, dated 1667, and William Robertson. These men were able and well-educated, typical of the wealthier tradesmen of the town who built up portfolios of property by lending money on mortgage to fellow shopkeepers in need of capital. They sent their sons to the Free School and, in some cases, to Oxford or Cambridge. They provided handsome dowries for their daughters. When their children came to marry, they had their lawyers arrange complex marriage settlements to ensure adequate provision for any children of the marriage. They served their turns as High Bailiff of the borough, except for John Prynn, who was fined at the manor court in 1711 for refusing to take office. When they died, they left bequests to the poor, many of which are listed on the board of benefactors still to be seen in the parish church.

The first known trade directory covering Halesowen is the *Universal British Directory*, published in 1792. The Halesowen entry, however, is confined to an account of the gardens at the Leasowes. The first to list tradesmen's names is Pigot's 1822 *Directory of Shropshire*. The 1835 directory gives the market day as Monday with fairs on the Mondays of Easter and Whitsun weeks. By 1868, the market day is given as Saturday and only the Easter fair is mentioned. In 1923 a corrugated-iron market hall was erected in the garden of John Hodgett's grocer's shop on Hagley Street. It served as the town's indoor market until the redevelopment of Hagley Street in the 1960s.

Apart from slight alterations to the road pattern in the turnpike era, the medieval layout of the borough of Halesowen remained intact until the comprehensive redevelopment of the town in the 1960s. The numbering adopted around 1900 for the older streets will be used in this description of the town. The line drawings show the street frontages as they appeared about 1950.

Great Cornbow

The high status merchants' houses on the south side of the market-place became known as 'Great Cornbow', referring to the chief commodity sold in the market and the bridge which carried the road from Bromsgrove over the Stour and into the town. When house numbers were applied to Great Cornbow about 1900, the lower numbers were given to the houses next to the Congregational Chapel on the corner of Hagley Street. This survey of properties will begin at Brooklands, the large house immediately to the west of Cornbow Bridge, which was numbered 9 Great Cornbow.

Brooklands probably began its existence as the miller's house at Cornbow Mill. It was purchased from Sir Thomas Lyttelton by Samuel Powell of Halesowen, timber merchant, and is mentioned in the settlement drawn up for the marriage of Powell's son, William, to Mary Butler in 1746.[8] By the time William Powell died in 1778, there was a malthouse on the site, probably converted from the mill. When William's son, Samuel Powell, died in 1807 the property passed to his daughter Sarah, who later married the Rev. John Garbett of Birmingham, clerk. By 1844, Garbett's property included a large three-storey house facing west, tenanted by George Kenwrick, surgeon, and the malting, occupied by Isaac Mallen, maltster, who later ran the *Half Moon* in Peckingham Street. Kenwrick was followed by two other doctors, Charles Bloxham and Daniel Weld Phillips. The house was later bought by Robert Smart of High Street, a cattle dealer, whose son-in-law, Richard Thomas Pearson, moved in and named the house 'Brooklands'. Pearson let the old mill building to the Salvation Army, who held their meetings there from around 1900.[9] The ruins of the mill could still be seen from Cornbow Bridge in the 1960s. Pearson was followed by Francis Harold Grove, button manufacturer, who died in 1944. By then, Brooklands had become the offices of the Halesowen and Hasbury Co-operative Society. It was demolished in about 1970 and replaced by modern offices for Barnardos.

Institute

Brooklands

The next building on Great Cornbow was the Halesowen Institute, Reading Room and Library, built in 1877 by John Skipworth Gibbons of the Leasowes on land bought from Robert Smart. The promoters would have had in mind the success of the Birmingham and Midland Institute and the high ideals of the mechanics institutes that were founded in most industrial towns at this time. The first secretaries were Arthur John Eaton and William Sluter. In 1925 John Skipworth Gibbons gave the Institute to a group of trustees on behalf of the people of Halesowen. The trustees were Frank Somers, John Benjamin Downing, Frank Tench Goodman,

36 *Great Cornbow, 1962, showing Brooklands, then owned by the Halesowen & Hasbury Industrial Co-operative Society, and the former Halesowen Institute, and occupied by Messrs Brady Brothers, leather goods manufacturers.*

17 18 19 20

35 *9-20 Great Cornbow, c.1950*

George Frederick Grove, Alfred Homfray, John Chapman and Eli Beard. By 1938, the Institute had lost popularity and the Charity Commissioners gave permission for its sale to Wilfred Harrison of Church Street, an electrical contractor. In 1948, Harrison sold the building to Ernest Brady, whose firm, Brady Brothers, made leather goods for the fishing tackle and gun trades. The building is now divided into offices and named 'Helen House', after Ernest Brady's daughter.

In 1900, the cottages in the alley next to the Institute were numbered 11-15 Great Cornbow. Rows of cottages at right angles to the street are typical of English market towns, where tradesmen often put up accommodation for their journeymen workers in the yards behind their shops. The proprietor lived at 16–18 Great Cornbow, once an imposing structure called the 'Bank House', presumably so named because of the slope of the street down to Cornbow Bridge. It was built of brick in the late

37 *16-20 Great Cornbow, 1949. The cottages on the left were demolished in the early 1950s and replaced by advertising hoardings. The swimming baths were built on the site in 1963.*

17th or early 18th century and had five large casement windows on the first floor, the second from the north situated above a generous brick archway that gave access to the yard behind. This was the home of William Wight whose name appears on the list of benefactors in Halesowen Church, having in 1614 charged these premises with the payment of 20s. annually to the poor of Halesowen. By 1746 the building, now divided into two houses, had been sold by the Rev. John Wight to Samuel Powell and was occupied by Thomas Taylor and Mary Harris, widow. In 1820, the Charity Commissioners noted that the 20s. was paid by Mrs Sarah Harris and distributed amongst the poor by the High Bailiff of the Borough on Good Friday, in sums of 6d., 4d. and 3d. each. By 1839, the houses were owned by Miss Powell and occupied by Benjamin Moore, tailor, and Thomas Hodgkins, nail manufacturer.[10] The property passed to Richard Pearson whose tenant for many years was Major Tildesley, haulier. The buildings were demolished in the early 1950s.

Next to 18 Great Cornbow was a large nail warehouse with a high central cart entrance. It was linked to number 19 on the west and was at one time rented by Thomas Hodgkins, chain and nail manufacturer. It later became part of the nail manufactory of Ephraim Ball. Until its demolition in the 1950s, it had a large sign above the entry 'Great Cornbow Works, P. Arden Thompson, Guest & Co Ltd., horse shoe manufacturers, iron and steel merchants, agricultural engineers'.

Number 19 Great Cornbow was a fine Georgian house of three storeys with rows of five sash windows on the first and second floors. According to the caption to a photograph in Halesowen Library, there was a brick in the door jamb incised 'BW 1762'. The initials may refer to the bricklayer rather than the owner, for it is likely that the house was built by John Bradley, who took over the tannery at Cornbow Bridge on the death of Thomas Sansom in the same year. John Bradley died in 1814 and was succeeded, both at the big house and at the tannery, by his son James. James Bradley died in 1829, and the family connection with the house ended with the death of his daughter Charlotte in 1846. It was at this time that Benjamin Trewolla, who ran the elegant drapery shop in High Street, came to live here. He died in 1870 and his widow sold the house to Ephraim Ball, who ran the nail manufactory at 20 Great Cornbow. Ephraim Ball died in 1884 but his widow

38 *19-20 Great Cornbow, 1957.*

39   *19 Great Cornbow, 1958. The windows over the entry were painted on to the brickwork to preserve the symmetry of the building. A brick beside the doorway was dated 1762.*

continued to live in the house which she called Cornbow House. The next owner was the solicitor, Alfred Hollowell, whose collection of antiques is referred to by Lena Schwarz in *The Halesowen Story*. The house was demolished about 1960.

Number 20 Great Cornbow was an ancient half-timbered structure with a tall jettied gable facing the street. The surviving deeds commence in 1693, when Henry Haden of Haden Hill sold the house to William Southall, of Pembroke College, Oxford.[11] The Southwells conveyed the house to Joseph Townsend of Halesowen, butcher, who sold to William Millward the younger of Halesowen maltster. Millward built a large malting on the land behind the house but went bankrupt in 1776. The premises were taken over by William Pardoe of Halesowen, baker and maltster, who died in 1836; his daughters Sarah and Elizabeth continued the business until the death of Sarah Pardoe in 1859, after which the house and building became a nail manufactory run by Ephraim Ball of Halesowen and John George Reay of Dudley, trading under the name of Guest & Co. When they bought the freehold of the factory in 1873 it included a warehouse, blacksmith's shop, engine house, nail shop, chimney stack, blacking shop, chain and iron warehouse, stables, sheds and other buildings. Ephraim Ball died in 1884 but Guest & Co. Ltd was continued by John George Reay, who moved to Rockingham Hall, Hagley. His manager on site, William Franklin, lived in the half-timbered house. When Guest & Co. sold the factory to Halesowen Borough Council in 1940, the directors were F.G. Thomson and Fred J.H. Thomson, and the Company Secretary was Walter Cyril Franklin. The Franklins were the last occupants of the house before its demolition in 1963. From 1940, Halesowen Borough Council used the yard behind the house to park refuse lorries.

Number 21 Great Cornbow was a large two-storey, brick-built house with a porch over the central doorway and three sash windows on the first floor. It is first mentioned in the 1669 will of Abraham Crane of Halesowen, draper, in which he

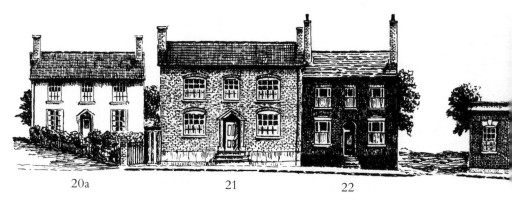

20a 21 22

40 *20a-27 Great Cornbow, c.1950*

leaves 'Broad Gates', a dwelling house in the Borough of Halesowen, to his brother John Crane. There is no evidence of the house having a separate cart entrance, let alone unusually broad gates, but it was adjacent to the gates of number 20 Great Cornbow. The distinctive name occurs again in 1807 when Charles William Bloxham, surgeon, mortgaged his house, 'Broad Gates', in Cornbow in the occupation of Edward Kenwrick, surgeon.[12] The house later belonged to George Granger, maltster, who was a deacon of the nearby Congregational Church. When Granger died in 1878, the church considered purchasing his house as a manse. Broad Gates was later the home of George Benjamin Hingley, John Holmes MD, and George Alexander Pryce, and subsequently became the offices of J. Rann Green, solicitor and clerk to the county magistrates for Halesowen. It was demolished about 1960.

Number 22 Great Cornbow was a smaller two-storey brick house with a central doorway. It was purchased in 1786 by William Day of Halesowen, a glazier whose gravestone can still be found in Halesowen churchyard. He was followed by his son Edward Green Day, named after his uncle, the wealthy nailmaster of Mucklow Hill. Edward's sister Frances left the house to Edward Moore of Halesowen, surgeon, who sold it to Daniel Weld Philips of Brooklands House, Cornbow.[13]

Number 24 Great Cornbow belonged in 1750 to William Barnsley, whitesmith, but in 1816 the house was purchased by the Birmingham solicitor, George Hinchliffe, who was a partner with Joseph Harris at the button manufactory in Peckingham Street.[14] The house had recently been occupied by Joseph Carruthers, another solicitor. Hinchliffe demolished the building and built the present three-storey brick house on the site. Either side of the front door he placed incised bricks reading 'GH 1817'. The house was purchased by William Hayes in 1854 and became known as Comberton House, after the picturesque Worcestershire village. It was let to a succession of doctors, including George Dunn, Hugh Ker, Thomas McLauchlan, Ernest Tathan and Daniel Weld Phillips, who bought the freehold. Other doctors who practised from Comberton House include Edward Walls, John Thompson, George Mold,

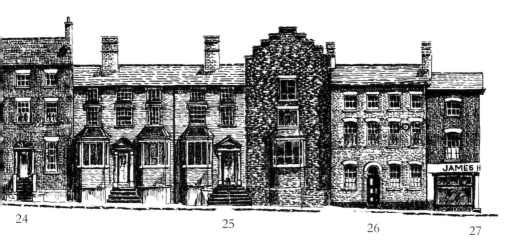

24   25   26   27

Herbert Bland, John Daly, A.S. MacVicar and G.T. Newton. Comberton House was bought by Halesowen Borough Council in 1952 and became the Treasurer's Department. The house now belongs to Dudley Metropolitan Borough.

Number 25 Great Cornbow is a very large three-storey building with five sash windows on the first and second floors and a three-storey gabled wing to the west with casement windows. The ground floor is symmetrical, with two imposing doorways, each with two bay windows either side. The façade probably dates from the early 19th century when this was the home of William Steel Hayes, Halesowen's leading solicitor. Hayes was born in Cheadle, Staffordshire, but, after his widowed mother Lydia married the solicitor George Hinchliffe, he was given a partnership in Hinchliffe's practice in Halesowen. William Steel Hayes died in 1857, after which

41   *Comberton House is on the left of this view of Great Cornbow, 1976.*

42   *3 Great Cornbow,*
1962, then occupied
by Percy S. Knight,
decorator.

his son William Hayes continued the practice, in partnership with Arthur Wright of Oldbury. His son, Arthur George Hayes, inherited the practice in 1879 and took in another partner, Samuel Goodman. Arthur George Hayes lived in Laurel Lane, and Hayes and Goodman occupied the new offices at 26 Great Cornbow. Number 25 Great Cornbow was purchased by another solicitor, John Wright, who continued his practice there until the Wright family sold the house to Halesowen Urban District Council in 1927. The new library and council chamber were built in the garden of this house in 1933. The building is still used as council offices by Dudley Metropolitan Borough.

Number 26 Great Cornbow is a three-storey brick building, which was built as public offices for the solicitor William Hayes in the 1860s. When William Hayes' original house was taken over by the solicitor John Wright, the 'Public Offices' became the premises of Hayes and Goodman. The partners in this firm were Arthur George Hayes, grandson of the founder, who lived at Grange Villas, Laurel Lane, and Samuel Goodman, who lived at Wolverleigh, 8 Hagley Road. They rented part of the 'Public Offices' to the new Halesowen Rural District Council, which held its meetings there from 1895-1901. The building then became known as the 'Old Public Offices'. Later partners in Hayes and Goodman included Alfred Homfray, of Otterbourne Court, Bundle Hill, Frederick Tench Goodman and Ronald Samuel Goodman. Some of the firm's records are now in the Record Office at Worcester.[15]

Numbers 27-9 Great Cornbow were small shops that were demolished in 1933 when the new library was built and Hagley Street widened. Albert Tolley's shop, formerly numbered 27 Great Cornbow, was rebuilt as a row of new shops on Hagley Street which included J.H. Hobbs' ironmonger's, D.V. Priest's radio and television shop and Raybold's baker's.

Opposite to the Council House stood number 3 Great Cornbow, a fine red-brick house with the date 1759 cut into a stone over the central dormer window. Its history dates back to at least 1622 when John Deeley of Lapal left his son Richard a 'house and smithy standing in the middle of Cornbow Street in the occupation of Roger Coley'. In 1769, it formed part of the settlement when John Cox of the borough of Halesowen, hingemaker, married Mary Smith of Halesowen, spinster.[16] Thomas Taylor of Halesowen, blacksmith, bought the freehold of the smithy in 1837.[17] From 1876, the property belonged to the Knight family of painters and decorators. The last occupant, in the 1960s, was Percy S. Knight.

Hagley Street

Hagley Street takes its name from the turnpike road from Birmingham to Hagley. When the Post Office allotted street numbers, the houses and shops on the east side of Hagley Street were numbered 1-17, from Peckingham Street to Laurel Lane. Most of these premises were small shops and cottages, which were demolished about 1930 to enable the widening of the road and to make way for the new library and council chamber. The west side of Hagley Road included a large public house and much bigger private houses and shops. It was numbered 18-35, from Hagley Road to High Street. The numbering system has not changed despite the rebuilding of all the shops from 24-35.

The first building on the west side of Hagley Street, numbered 18, was the *Bull's Head Inn*. It was part of a large complex of houses and business premises belonging to Walter Woodcock. His tenant at the *Bull's Head* in 1784 was Daniel Willetts. In a sale of the Woodcock's estate in 1827, it was described as 'All that well accustomed public house known by the sign of the Bull's Head situate in Hagley Street in Halesowen … in the occupation of Edward Tranter'. It was purchased by John Smith who was the host until the 1880s, when his daughter, Sarah Miles, took over. The *Bull's Head* was rebuilt about 1900 with a central timbered gable and a bay window on the first floor. Successive publicans included Alfred Micklewright, John Frank Wareing, Thomas Clews, Deveril Hill, Samuel Douglas Millsum and Frederick Smith. The *Bull's Head* was demolished in 1962 to be replaced by a block of three shops and offices called Churchill House.

Number 19 Hagley Street was a low two-storey house with three sash windows on the first floor. For many years it was a confectioner's shop run by Harry Holloway and, later, by Lillian Weston. It was latterly a café but was demolished to make way for Churchill House.

Number 20 Hagley Street was a three-storey house built in the early 19th century. Behind it stood a large malting, which, according to the sale catalogue of 1827, was occupied by Joseph Taylor and was capable of making about 3,000 bushels of malt per annum. The house and malting had been bought by Joseph Taylor,

43 The Bull's Head Inn, *Hagley Street, 1962. The pub was here barely 60 years old, having been rebuilt about 1900 to reduce the angle of Hagley Street and Hagley Road.*

maltster, for £260.[18] In 1847 Joseph Taylor sold the house to George Moseley who kept the *Globe Inn*, Peckingham Street. At this time the malting was occupied by William Ganner, another maltster who had been the landlord of the *Queen's Head* in Birmingham Street. Three generations of the Moseley family ran a butcher's business at Number 20 Hagley Street. They were followed by Charles Homer and, latterly, George Bridge.

Numbers 21-2 Hagley Street was a three-storey house with four sash windows on the first and second floors. It was also part of the Woodcock estate. Number 21 was for many years a grocer's shop run by Thomas Hunt, but it later became a bookshop run by A.H. Hill, who had been an English teacher at Halesowen Grammar School from 1912-41; number 22 was a furniture shop run by Barzilla

44   *18-35 Hagley Street, c.1950*

45 *Hagley Street from Summer Hill, 1955.*

Williams, who emigrated to Salt Lake City. It was later a draper's shop run by Nellie Robinson, Joseph Robinson, Fanny Goodman, Annie McNaught and Mary Moseley; this building still stands.

The next buildings on Hagley Street were a nail warehouse and a malting, which in 1827 was said to be capable of making about 4,000 bushels of malt per annum. Lloyds Bank was built on this site in 1876, and was numbered 23 Hagley Street. The early managers were David Nutt, Henry Maxon, Norman William Harrison and Robert Clive Ralphs. Lloyds Bank moved to new premises in High Street, and the imposing Victorian bank on Hagley Street is now an amusement arcade.

Number 24 Hagley Street was a handsome three-bay house with a shallow front garden protected by iron railings. This house had belonged to Sir Thomas Lyttelton and was occupied by his agent, Walter Woodcock, who died in 1736. In 1740 Woodcock's son, Walter, moved up in local society by marrying Frances,

26   28   29   30   31   32   33   34   35

46   *Hagley Street from Great Cornbow, 1955.*

daughter of William Lea of Halesowen Grange. He died in 1801, leaving most of his property, including the house and maltings on Hagley Street, to his son Walter. Walter had married his cousin Frances, daughter of William Smith of Halesowen Grange, and now lived at Dove House Fields Farm, Hunnington. The big house in Hagley Street was occupied by his sister, Elizabeth, widow of one of Halesowen's leading nailmasters, John Green. When Walter Woodcock died in 1821, his property had to be divided among his six sisters and their husbands, and their wrangling led to the great sale of 1827. Elizabeth Green's son, John Green, a very opulent nailmaster, continued to live at Hagley Street until his death in 1869. The Green family moved away from Halesowen but continued to own the house, which was converted to a grocery shop by Charles John Peach. The house remained a grocer's shop until its demolition and replacement with the new Co-operative superstore, which opened in May 1965.

Numbers 26-7 Hagley Street was a large, cement-rendered, two-storey house, with two dormer widows giving light to the attics. It had formed part of the estate of John Brettell, a local maltster who died in 1744. Brettell's widow Mary married a local saddler called Josiah Green, whose father was also a wealthy maltster and whose brothers were the talented artists, James and Benjamin Green. By the early 19th century, the house had been divided into two parts, one a public house called the *Black Swan*, occupied by Sarah Edmiston, and the other a post office, also run by Mrs Edmiston. She was the occupant in 1825 when the Green family sold the house to John Skidmore, grocer.[19] Sarah Edmiston was followed as postmistress by Frances Cox, who continued until about 1841. The house then became a butcher's shop run successively by William Jeptha, William Hollies and William Robinson. About 1900, when it was numbered 26 Hagley Street, it was purchased by Harry Parkes, the well-known printer and stationer. It remained in the ownership of H. Parkes Ltd until its demolition about 1965. The right-hand side of the building, 27 Hagley Street, was once a greengrocer's shop run by Edward, and then Charles, Grainger, but it was later incorporated into the stationery shop.

Numbers 28-9 Hagley Street was a single house with a large malting behind. It too had formed part of John Brettell's estate and had passed to the Green family. It was sold in 1825 to John Bissell, maltster, whose executors sold it to William Jones.[20] William and his son Edward Jones continued the malting business until the 1880s. The house was then rebuilt as two shops. The first, numbered 28 Hagley Street, was an elegant brick-built, three-storey building, with a tall gable facing the street. It had two arched sash windows on the first floor and a three-light Venetian window on the second floor and was for many years a shoe shop run by John Thomas Taylor. The other, 29 Hagley Street, was a three-storey house with two bay windows on the first floor overlooking the street. This now became the Halesowen Coffee House Company Limited, a more sober alternative to the public house, managed by Thomas Smart, Secretary of Birmingham Street Primitive

47   *28-32 Hagley Street, 1958.*

Methodist Church. The building was later bought by Harry Parkes and occupied by Granville Hawkeswood the draper.

Numbers 30-2 Hagley Street was an imposing three-storey, cement-rendered house with rows of six sash windows on the first and second floors. The roof was partly hidden behind a parapet. This house had passed to the Green family from John Brettell. The principal tenants during much of the 18th century were Thomas Oldbury, who died in 1813, and his son Thomas Oldbury, who died in 1815. The Oldburys often held alehouse licences, suggesting that this may have been an inn. By 1825 the building was occupied by a grocer named William Horton, who had purchased the freehold at the sale of the Greens' property;[21] after he died in 1855, part of the house became an ironmonger's, run successively by John Booth and Alfred Pagett. It was numbered 30 Hagley Street. More recently it was a greengrocer's shop run by R. Willetts. Another part of the house, 31 Hagley Street, was for many years occupied by Chilton Brothers, drapers, and subsequently by a laundry company called the Valeting Service. By 1908, the whole building had been purchased by a chemist named Adam Lawton, who occupied number 32 Hagley Street, the largest of the three shops. There are stained glass windows in the church to the memory of Adam Lawton and his wife Lydia. Lawton was succeeded by Cass & Company, chemists, and later by Marsh & Baxter, the butchers.

Between numbers 32 and 33 Hagley Street was an entrance to a yard of three cottages sometimes known as Chip Yard. In 1923 a large metal building was erected in this yard which served as Halesowen's indoor market until 1960. Number 33 Hagley Street was a three-storey house with a cement-rendered façade. The property appears to have been part of the Green family holding, for it is referred to in 1825 in the deeds to 32 Hagley Street as having been sold to Thomas Edge. Along with his partner Aaron Rose, Thomas Edge ran a gun-barrel manufactory at the former slitting mill at the bottom of Mucklow Hill. His tenant in Hagley Street was a draper named Henry Fernie. Thomas Edge died in 1841, leaving the house to his daughter Mary. The premises were for many years occupied by a grocer named John Hodgetts. In about 1923, the shop was taken over by George Mason, who already had a grocery business at 22 Peckingham Street.

Number 34 Hagley Street was a two-storey brick-built house, with a shop front and cart entrance on the ground floor and three sash windows on the second floor. Thomas Poole of Halesowen, shopkeeper, left the house to his nephew Thomas Jones in his will of 1808. It later belonged to Joseph Brettell, but by 1850 it was a grocer's shop run first by John Clay and then by Isaac Boswell. In 1881 it was taken over by Thomas Yarnold, a baker and confectioner. The next proprietor was Thomas Smart, also a confectioner, who was Secretary of Birmingham Street Primitive Methodist Church and President of the Halesowen and Hasbury Industrial Co-operative Society. The shop became the Halesowen and Hasbury Industrial Co-operative Society's confectionery department until rebuilt by the Society in 1962. At this time, the Halesowen and Hasbury Labour Club, whose premises were above the shop, moved to new premises on Hagley Road.

The last house in Hagley Street was number 35, a two-storey brick building with two attic windows in the roof. It, too, belonged to Thomas Poole and then to Joseph Brettell. Brettell's tenant was a shoemaker named John Glaze. He was succeeded by Joseph Finney, a master shoemaker, who in 1851 employed five journeymen. From about 1860 to 1900, the house was occupied by Joseph Nock, a farmer, butcher and greengrocer, and proprietor of the concert hall in Peckingham Street. The premises were then owned by William Sluter, one of Halesowen's early historians, and occupied by the china and glass dealer, Walter Seeley. Like his neighbour Thomas Smart, Seeley was a strong supporter of Birmingham Street Primitive Methodist Church. His business was later continued by his widow, Alice Seeley. Number 35 Hagley Street was demolished in the 1950s, the site remaining vacant until the rebuilding of the Co-operative confectionery shop in 1962.

High Street

High Street originally extended from the church down the hill to Laconstone Bridge, passing the junctions of Peckingham Street and Great Cornbow, and terminating at the corner where the road to Hagley left the town. Soon after the Birmingham to Hagley road was turnpiked, its route into the town was diverted at Rumbow, along the line of the now culverted Laconstone Brook, to enter the town at the junction of High Street and Peckingham Street. The part of the High Street that had become part of the turnpike road gradually became known as Hagley Street. Premises on the west side of High Street were numbered 1-19, from Hagley Street to Church Street, and those on the east side were numbered 20-39, from Church Street to Hagley Street. In the 1960s, however, Church Street was subsumed in High Street. The enlarged High Street was re-numbered with even numbers (2-84) on the west and odd numbers (1-91) on the east, both running from Stourbridge Road to Hagley Street.

Laconstone House, which stood on a culvert over the Laconstone Brook, was numbered 1 High Street. The earliest deed traced so far is a conveyance of 1739,[22] but from 1839 the house was a draper's shop, run successively by Benjamin Trewolla and his son Richard. Bate & Winzer later held these premises, and were followed by W.S. Welch and Son.[23] Laconstone House was demolished and replaced by Finefare, Halesowen's first supermarket, which opened in June 1962.

Numbers 2 and 3 High Street were one large house with four sash windows on the first floor. From 1828,

48   *W.S Welch & Son Ltd, High Street, 1958.*

49   *1-19 High Street, c.1950.*

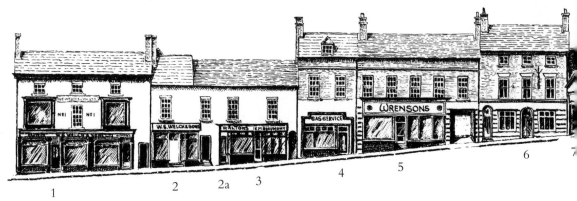

the southern half was a butcher's shop run by Joseph Smart and then by his son Robert. This shop was later taken over by W.S. Welch & Son, who extended their drapery store into this part of the building. Number 3 High Street was also a draper's shop, run latterly by Mrs Beaumont. Both shops were demolished to build the Finefare Supermarket and Foster Brothers menswear shop in 1962.

Numbers 4-5 High Street was an old established grocer's shop, run from 1840 by Elijah Thompson & Sons. By the 1950s this family business had become part of a chain of grocery stores owned by Wrenson's Ltd. The shop had an elaborate network of cables, that enabled each assistant to propel a brass container carrying a customer's bill to a centrally positioned cashier.

50   *Wrenson's grocery store, High Street, 1958.*

The next building in High Street was a Victorian house built on the site of the ancient *Lyttelton Arms Inn* (see plate 71, p.84). The house later became a greengrocer's with a beerhouse licence. It was then named the *Old Lyttelton Arms* to distinguish it from the public house on the opposite side of the High Street which had taken over the original name.

Next to the *Old Lyttelton Arms* were two small houses, 7-8 High Street, which were

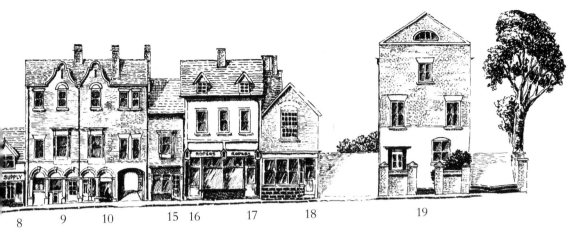

owned from 1896 by Campbell Simeon Drayton, a watchmaker and jeweller. His business was continued by his son, James Lewis Drayton. Prior to their demolition in the mid-1960s, these shops were occupied by Dewhurst's the butchers and the Boot Supply Co.

The next house on the High Street was numbered 9-10 and was rebuilt about 1890 to become the town's new Post Office. The building had a large archway to the right leading to a yard and a private road into the Highfield. The history of the property is linked to that of the Carpenter family, who owned it at least as early as 1648. In that year John Carpenter, a shoemaker of Halesowen and son of Thomas Carpenter of Stoke Prior, married Joan, daughter of Thomas Jackson of Halesowen,

51 *The Post Office, High Street, 1958.*

yeoman. Provision was made for the children of this marriage, with the Carpenters pledging the house in High Street and the Jacksons giving a dowry of £40.[24] The marriage was indeed a success, for, in 1675, the eldest child, John, was sent to Pembroke College, Oxford and became vicar of Broxted in Essex. The Rev. John Carpenter did not lose touch with Halesowen, however, for his daughter Sarah married Thomas Wight of Halesowen, baker, in 1712. In 1686 the second son, Jonathan Carpenter, also a shoemaker, married Margaret, daughter of William Robertson, of Halesowen, mercer. The marriage settlement mentioned the same premises in High Street, but on this occasion the dowry was £80. Jonathan Carpenter also prospered, for he could afford to send his elder son Jonathan to Pembroke College, Oxford in 1709 and his younger son John to Merton College in 1713. Jonathan Carpenter became vicar of Sheldon in Warwickshire, and John Carpenter became vicar of Pagham in Sussex. Jonathan Carpenter, the shoemaker, died in 1726, charging his house in the High Street with the payment of 20s. per annum, to be distributed among 20 of the poorest inhabitants of Halesowen on 2 February each year.

The executors of the Rev. Jonathan Carpenter sold the house in High Street to Thomas Wight in 1761. The property then descended with the Wight's house on the other side of High Street until the whole estate was sold at auction in 1829. The Carpenters' house now became a butcher's shop, run for many years by William Hollies. Some of the buildings in the yard at the back became cottages, later numbered 11-14 High Street. By 1884 the whole property had been purchased by Thomas Hodgetts, Halesowen's postmaster, who was Chairman of the Rural District Council in 1903 and 1917. He rebuilt the house with the town's new Post Office on the left and a chemist's shop on the right, occupied successively by Alfred Glasspool, Thomas Cooper, George Masson and D.H.Haines.

Number 15 High Street was, for many years, a bakery run by Ernest Ploughman. The entrance to 16-17 High Street was once approached by steep steps, but the doorway was later brought down to street level. The house was a haberdasher's, run by Annie Roper and, later, by Sydney Shacklock. Number 18 High Street was latterly occupied by Richard Willetts, a greengrocer. Number 19 High Street was an old building called Church Steps House, easily identified from its deeds, as it was always described as bordering the churchyard on the north. The list of benefactors in the church includes the name of Richard Dickins, who, in 1640, gave an annuity of 6s. 8d. to the church, to be paid at Easter, and 10s. to the poor of the borough

Rectory   20   24   24a   25

52   *20-39 High Street, c.1950.*

of Halesowen, to be given on St Thomas' day, both charged on his house by the churchyard. Church Steps House was later the home of Josiah Gaunt, Halesowen's barber-surgeon, who died in 1811. More recently it was the office of the solicitors Ernest Harry Grove and Francis Howard Grove respectively. It was purchased by Halesowen Borough Council and demolished in 1963.[25]

The numbering on the opposite side of High Street began with number 20, an old established public house called the *Leopard Inn*, which stood next to the Vicarage. The *Leopard Inn* lost its licence about 1906 and became a hairdresser's operated by William Hall. In around 1940, the premises were rebuilt as a branch of the Birmingham Municipal Bank. The building was re-numbered 65 High Street in the 1960s and is currently a betting shop.

53 *Church Steps House, High Street, 1957. The cottages behind were known as Gaunt's Yard after Josiah Gaunt of Church Steps House, who died in 1811.*

Numbers 21-23 High Street were allotted to three cottages which stood in the yard of the *Leopard Inn*. Number 24 High Street was a large house with two gables facing the street. From 1618 to 1798 it was the home of the Wight family, farmers and bakers, who were probably related to the Wights who ran the tannery in Great Cornbow.[26] After the death of Thomas Wight in 1798, the house was occupied by Joseph Carruthers, an attorney, who had married Elizabeth, daughter of Ferdinando Smith of the Grange. From 1896 the house was a tailor's shop, owned by John Arthur Young and his

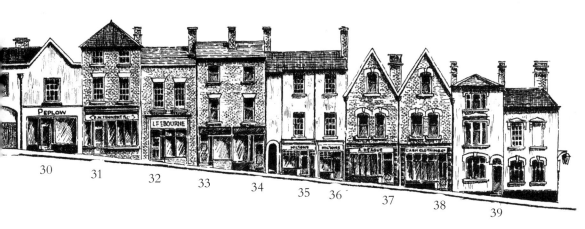

30   31   32   33   34   35   36   37   38   39

54 *Apollo Stores is situated on the far left of this picture of the High Street, 1958.*

brother Osmond Young. More recently it was occupied by Dearne and Raistrick, wireless engineers and, later, by Fowlers Television. It was demolished in the 1960s.

Numbers 25-6 High Street was a large three-storey, double-fronted house with an entry to a yard on the south side. The property belonged to Lord Lyttelton, who sold it to Joseph Harris, the button manufacturer, in 1839.[27] The premises were occupied by Joseph Harris's son, William Harris, a stationer and printer, who published a popular history of Halesowen in 1836. William Harris died in 1885, but his executors did not sell the property until 1919, by which time it was a grocer's shop called the Apollo Stores, run by Major Hackett. The shop survived until the mid-1960s as a branch of Messrs Wimbush, confectioners. Numbers 27-9 were allotted to three cottages in the yard behind, sometimes called Old Post Office Yard.

Number 30 High Street was a timber-framed house with one gable facing the street. This, too, was owned by Joseph Harris, who died in 1845. It was occupied by Jane Hodgetts and her son Thomas. Thomas Hodgetts later became Halesowen's postmaster and ran the Post Office from these premises, until moving to the new Post Office on the other side of the street about 1884. More recently it was a branch of the Stourbridge jewellery business, run by William Henry Peplow. It was re-numbered 75 High Street in the 1960s and is now called Easter Interiors.

Number 31 High Street was a three-storey brick house with good quality sash windows, dating from the late 18th or early 19th century. It had a malting on the land at the rear, sloping down to Birmingham Road. In his will of 1842, Joseph Harris left the house to his son James Harris, a maltster. It was subsequently purchased by John Burr, the gun-barrel manufacturer, and occupied by a tailor named John Wade. By 1900 it had become a chemist's shop, run successively by Frederick John Lane, John William Cass, Arthur Edward Kennerley and Edward William Tennent. It is now numbered 77 High Street and is occupied by Dixons the estate agents.

Number 32 High Street was a two-storey early 19th-century house which also belonged to John Burr. From the 1860s it was occupied by a greengrocer called James Bagley, whose wife, Anne, and his daughter, Emily, continued the business until the Second World War. By 1960, the shop was run by L.F. Ebourne, florist and fruiterer. The building is still standing, numbered 79 High Street and is currently occupied by a Cancer Research charity shop.

The next building in High Street was a three-storey house divided into two shops, which belonged to John Burr. Number 33 was a saddler's shop, occupied successively by Elizabeth Reynolds, John Hay, William John Butler and Ambrose Sturman. Number 34 was inhabited by a shoemaker called Robert Williams. The shop was later run as an ironmonger's by his widow Sophia and by his son, Edward Williams, who bought the freehold of the shops from the Burr family. The last member of the family to run the business was Clifford Williams. The site of these shops is now occupied by Poundbase and a branch of Lloyds Bank.

Numbers 35-6 High Street was an early 19th-century house divided into two shops, with a narrow entry to the north. It belonged to a tailor called Benjamin Brettell, one of the founders of the Congregational Church in 1811. By 1835, Number 35 was occupied by Thomas and James Bissell, who were nail ironmongers at Webb's Green and grocers and drapers in High Street. The mix of trades suggests that the Bissells may have encouraged their outworkers to take goods from the shop in lieu of wages. The grocery shop was continued by Jabez Percival Conduit and then became a branch of Charles Peach's grocery business (based at 24 Hagley Street). The shop was later run by Horace William Homer, a fishmonger, who was followed by Anne Russell, draper. Number 36 was once a beerhouse called *The Bell*, became a haberdasher's run by Charles Glaze and then a tailor's with Alfred Lewis as the proprietor. W.H. Peplow occupied the premises before moving to 30 High Street. By 1935 the shop had been bought by Frederick Boswell, a boot and shoe dealer from Old Hill. Stephen Hilton & Sons later moved here from 1 Hagley Street. The site is now occupied by Lloyds Bank.

Numbers 37-8 High Street were two shops owned by the Misses Carruthers, daughters of the local solicitor Joseph Carruthers. The shops were rebuilt in the late 19th century, probably by Mitchells & Butlers, with two prominent gables facing the street. Number 37 was a shoemaker's, run in turn by James Leech, Edward Leech, Richard Tildesley, and John Glaze. It was then run as a confectioner's by George Simmonds, James Ferriday, Walter Heague and his widow, Ada Heague, and later became a newsagent's and card shop. It is now Options Hairdressers. Number 38 High Street was a shoemaker's occupied by Jesse Smith and, later, John Eden. By 1908 it had become

55 Lyttelton Arms, *High Street, 1965.*

the Cash Clothing Company, 'Halesowen's cheapest shop', which was managed successively by Robert Jones, James Mitchell and Alfred Meakin. The shop was re-numbered as 89 High Street in the 1960s and is currently occupied by Now Secure Direct Finance.

The Misses Carruthers also owned the last house in High Street, occupied by Samuel White, a farmer and beer seller. When the original *Lyttelton Arms* closed down in 1845, Samuel White obtained a full licence for his house and called it the *Lyttelton Arms*. Later publicans include Benjamin Connop, Thomas Frederick Wood and Frank Bolus. Mitchells and Butlers had added the *Lyttelton Arms* to their chain by 1908, when William Pick was the host. He was followed by William James Pick. The pub has since become 89 High Street and has recently been renamed as *Picks*.

1-11 Peckingham Street

There is little sign of medieval town planning in Peckingham Street. The narrow building plots on the north side of the street go back either to the Laconstone Brook (culverted under Birmingham Road in the mid-18th century), or to the back yards of the houses in Birmingham Street. The houses on the south side of Peckingham Street are even more confined and may be encroachments on the market-place laid out by the Abbot of Hales in the 13th century. The earliest form of the street name found in court rolls or in property deeds is 'Prickingham Street', but there is no similar local place-name, surname or occupation which might be the origin of this unusual name. The houses on the north side were numbered 1-11 in about 1900, climbing up from Birmingham Road to Birmingham Street, and 12-22 going down the south side from the Bull Ring to Hagley Street.

Number 1 Peckingham Street was long associated with the Fiddian family who were tanners, saddlers and hinge makers in the 18th and 19th centuries. The water

9   10

11

56 *1-11 Peckingham Street, c.1950.*

running down the Laconstone Brook would have been vital in their trade and, when the stream was culverted under the newly constructed Birmingham Road, their outbuildings became a separate property on the new road. Barzilla Fiddian, a hinge maker, died in 1806, and his brother Richard Fiddian, a collar maker, died in 1835. From 1850, their premises were occupied by William Robertson, a butcher, who was followed by his son, also William Robertson. They were later occupied by George Edward Smart, an umbrella manufacturer, and then became a tobacconist's shop, run successively by Benjamin Law, Charles H. Johnson, and G. Widdowson.

Numbers 2 and 3 Peckingham Street were probably also owned by the Fiddians, for they later belonged to another hinge maker called James Hardeman. They then formed part of the property of Joseph Nock, and, after his death in 1906, they were purchased by Mary Ann Priest. The premises were rebuilt in the Victorian period with a three-storey façade and two hooded sash windows on the first floor. In 1881, number 2 was occupied by a tailor named Alfred Lewis, and after that by Herbert Lewis; it was later a confectioner's shop run by Giovanni Rosa. Number 3 Peckingham Street was a coffee house run by Thomas Smart, before he moved to Hagley Street in 1883. It was then a tobacconist's run by Naboth Priest. The business was continued by Mary Ann Priest until the 1920s when it was taken over by Harold Green as a grocer's shop.

Number 4 Peckingham Street was the *Golden Cross Inn*, which closed as a public house in 1906 (see plate 76, p.90). The last owner, Joseph Nock, started a music hall in a large outbuilding at the back of the pub about 1900. The premises were rebuilt in 1911 and, from 1919, the music hall became the Cosy Corner Cinema.[28] The site is now occupied by F.W. Woolworth & Co.

Number 5 Peckingham Street was a small shop that was absorbed into the Cosy Corner Cinema in about 1919. Numbers 6-7 Peckingham Street was

57 *Peckingham Street, 1954.*

58   *The former Cosy Corner Cinema, Peckingham Street, c.1950.*

a two-storey house with a cart entrance on the left, leading to a yard at the rear. Like the neighbouring *Golden Cross Inn*, the building belonged by the Male family and then to Thomas Bate.[29] From 1835 Bate's tenant was John Glaze, a boot and shoe maker, who ran a shoe factory at the rear. The house belonged to Reuben Parsons, a greengrocer, and later to Ann Parsons, his widow. Number 6 was later Hackett's the butchers and number 7, Moyle's the grocers. The site is now occupied by Boots the Chemists.

Number 8 Peckingham Street was an old-established inn called the *Half Moon*. It was a three-storey building with two sashed bay windows on the first floor. Charles Tomlins was the publican from 1809 until his death in 1827; it was then owned by Margaret and William Tomlins. From 1841 it was run by Joseph Hinton, Isaac Mallin, Rebecca Mallin, William Hollies, and Joseph Hipkiss in turn. In its later years it was known as the *Talbot Inn* and was run by Benjamin Grove, Daniel Parsons and Frank Bolus.[30] After its closure as a public house in 1906 it became a hairdresser's, run by James Cookson Phillips.

59   *Halesowen & Hasbury Industrial Co-operative Society, Peckingham Street, 1961.*

60 *The Co-operative Drapery Store, Birmingham Street, 1962.*

The deeds to 9 Peckingham Street date back to the 1660 will of William Wight of Cornbow, who left two houses in Peckingham Street as an endowment for the Free School. In the 19th century, these premises were leased by the Grammar School to David Phillips. In 1868 they were occupied by a grocer called Henry Symons Tucker, but by 1876 his shop had been taken over by the Halesowen and Hasbury Industrial Co-operative Society, with George Moyle as its first manager. The large three-storey building, which still stands, probably dates from this time. Co-operative societies had a political, as well as a commercial, purpose. The next manager, Benjamin Marsland, was a member of Birmingham Street Primitive Methodist Church and a well known local preacher. He was elected a councillor in 1904 and was Chairman of Halesowen Rural District Council in 1906 and 1910-11. The former Co-operative store is now occupied by a hairdresser and a herbal medicine shop.

The rival Lye Co-operative Society (later styled the Halesowen & District Prudential Co-operative Society) opened a shop at nearby 87 Birmingham Street about 1876. The premises had formerly been a factory where William Henry Rose employed about eight men making shovels. The first two managers of the Lye Co-operative shop were Ezra Crampton and John Farmer. This Society merged with the Halesowen and Hasbury Industrial Co-operative Society about 1900, and the shop at the top of Birmingham Street became the drapery department. The premises to the rear of the shop were used as a bakery until replaced in 1929 by the new model bakery on Bromsgrove Road. The drapery shop was vacated in 1965

61 *The Halesowen & Hasbury Industrial Co-operative Society bakery, behind the drapery store in Little Cornbow, c.1910.*

when the new Co-operative store on Hagley Street was opened. The vacant shop was used from 1967 to 1969 by Dancer's Ltd while their premises, at the bottom of Peckingham Street, were redeveloped. It was demolished soon after.

The imposing three-storey shop at the corner of Peckingham Street and Birmingham Street was sometimes numbered 11 Peckingham Street. From 1822 it was owned by David Phillips, a grocer and draper. The business was continued as a grocery shop by Edward Eyles, and then as a draper's by Benjamin White. Although remaining in White's ownership, the draper's shop was then occupied by Bate and Winzer, and later by James Talbot. About 1932 it became a greengrocer's run by Annie Granger, and it was later taken over by Byng and Knight as a hardware shop. It is now a branch of Lloyds the Chemists.

The Bull Ring

At the junction of Peckingham Street, Birmingham Street and Little Cornbow there was a large space known as the Bull Ring. This had probably been the principal market area of the town and was the site of some of its oldest inns. In 1822 the *Queen's Head Inn*, later 1 Birmingham Street, belonged to William Ganner, who was also the tenant of a malting on Hagley Street. His widow, Jane Ganner, still held the licence in 1850. Subsequent licensees included Charles Cox, Joseph Deeley, James Wakefield, Harry Whittle, Joseph Moore and Percy Withers. The pub eventually became a Davenport's house and is still in business.

62 Queen's Head Inn, *Birmingham Street, 1957.*

There was an isolated group of buildings in the middle of the Bull Ring including the *Star Inn*, formerly known as the *Red Cow*. For much of the 19th century, the *Star Inn* belonged to a grocer and beer seller named William Nash, and then to his son-in-law John Corbett. Subsequent licensees here were Mary Nash, William White, Edward Willetts, Thomas Hill, Benjamin Grove, Albert Henry Flavell, William Grainger, George Grainger, Alfred Marson, Alice Marson, Joseph Turner and J. Pardoe. John Corbett also owned the old shop adjoining the *Star Inn*, which

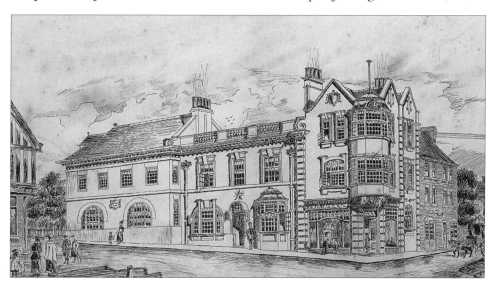

63 *Architect's impression of the Bull Ring, 1911.*

64   *4 Bull Ring, 1957, better known as Cross House and later as the Bethel Mission.*

was oddly numbered 45 Little Cornbow, or 45 Peckingham Street. It formed part of an ambitious project to redevelop the Bull Ring, promoted by Thomas Hartshorne of Netherton. In 1907 he commissioned the local architect, A.T. Butler, to draw up a scheme for building a new shop with a flat over it on the corner of the Bull Ring, improving the neighbouring *Star Inn*, and converting the large adjoining house, number 4 Bull Ring, into the Conservative Club. The shop, when completed, was the most elegant in Halesowen, featuring an oriel window over the door and a 1907 datestone. The new shop was occupied by Elizabeth Cook, draper, but it was later let to Polly Dunn, whose well known hairdressing establishment was called 'Maison Hetty'.

To the east of the *Star Inn*, and numbered 4 Bull Ring, was one of Halesowen's finest 18th-century houses. It was sometimes known as 'Cross House', after the old market cross which stood on the pavement south of the building. The cross blew down in a storm in 1908, and was re-erected in the churchyard. The house had belonged to the opulent Robertson family, four generations of whom were mercers and grocers in the town in the 17th and 18th centuries. William Robertson the elder, mercer, whose trade token has already been mentioned, was High Bailiff of Halesowen in 1689. Robert, son of Robert Robertson, of Halesowen, mercer, was born in 1763 and matriculated at Magdalen Hall, Oxford in 1782. He became curate of Harborne and master of Halesowen Free School from 1796 until his death in 1824.

In 1827, Cross House was bought from Robertson's executors by Henry Hodgetts, a butcher and cattle dealer. He also purchased property on the corner of Birmingham Street for his slaughterhouse, stables and coach house. Cross House was later occupied by

Hodgetts' son-in-law, Henry Hollies, also a butcher. It was sold in 1873 to Sarah Royston, alias Wakefield, a fishmonger. Sarah Wakefield's son, James Wakefield, became a music hall performer and she and her daughter, Sarah Ann Freeman, later described themselves as 'wardrobe dealers'. Thomas Hartshorne bought Cross House from Sarah Wakefield in 1900. The 1907 architect's drawing shows two distinctive arched windows on the north side of the ground floor and a plaque on which is the word 'club'. These features were probably for the benefit of the Conservative Club, which was based here from about 1904-10. The house was later known as the Bethel Mission, after a breakaway group from the Baptist Church, who held their services there in the 1930s. It was later rented by Worcestershire County Council for the Registrar of Births, Marriages

65 *The Old Market Cross in the Bull Ring, c.1900.*

and Deaths, and in 1949 was let to the Ministry of Works as a National Insurance Benefits Office. In 1965, Halesowen Borough Council bought the Bethel Mission, the *Star Inn* and 'Maison Hetty' from Thomas Hartshorne's granddaughter, Clarice Elizabeth Foley, for £12,500. Rooms in the Bethel Mission were let to the W.V.S. and St John Ambulance Brigade, whilst the *Star Inn* became a coffee bar. The whole complex of buildings was demolished in around 1970.

12-23 Peckingham Street

At the junction of the Bull Ring and the south side of Peckingham Street was an ancient inn called the *Talbot*, bequeathed in the 1651 will of William Attwood of Halesowen, whitesmith, to his son John Attwood. It ceased to be an inn in 1701 when it was bought by Robert Robinson of Halesowen, baker. In 1800 the premises were purchased by Joseph Harris and George Hinchliffe and used as a button factory.[31] When Joseph Harris moved his factory to Birmingham Street in 1825, the house was bought by Benjamin White, whose family later ran a grocery business there. This was taken over in about 1881 by William Hollies, butcher and cattle dealer. His premises were numbered 12-13 Peckingham Street. The business was continued as E.W. Hollies & Son right up until the redevelopment of this area in the 1960s.

A Halesowen Library photograph of the next building, number 15 Peckingham Street, is entitled 'old houses dated 1685'. This house had a tall gable facing the street. For many years it belonged to Walter Woodcock and formed Lot 15 in the 1827 sale of his property. It was described as a 'messuage used as a public house and known by the sign of the Dog & Duck situate in Peckingham Street, in Halesowen aforesaid, with two small tenements adjoining, and the outbuildings and appurtenances, now in the occupation of George Moseley and W. White.' The purchaser was George Moseley, who changed the name to the *Globe Tavern*. George Moseley was succeeded as publican by John Moseley, Martha Smith, Henry Russell, William Lea, and Elizabeth Lea. By 1912, the *Globe* had been taken over by Joseph Cooper & Co., who ran a small brewery near the *Malt Shovel* in Church Street. From 1940 it was run by Frederick Pardoe as a wine and spirit merchant's.

George Moseley bought several shops in Peckingham Street at the 1827 sale. One of them, later 16 Peckingham Street, was a butcher's shop, run by Prowse and Humphries and later by Alice Harris. It was later an office of Jack Bowen & Co, estate agents. Number 17 Peckingham Street was a shoe repair shop run by Clifford Allport and after that by A.M. Bannister.

Numbers 19-21 Peckingham Street were a row of two-storey shops, refronted by John Dancer in about 1890, with four sash windows to the first floor. Numbers 19-20 were run from the 1850s by Joseph Williams and his family, who were greengrocers and, later, fishmongers. By 1908, the shops were owned by John Dancer, who leased 21 Peckingham Street to Richard Marsh, butcher.

The deeds to the block of shops at the bottom of Peckingham Street go back to 1657 when Richard Maggs of Halesowen, butcher, sold a barn and land at 'Prickingham Street' to Richard Bodiley of Halesowen, ironmonger. By the 18th century the barn had been converted into cottages, which, in 1776, were sold by

66 *12-23 Peckingham Street, c.1950.*

67   *William Hollies butcher's shop, Peckingham Street, c.1900.*

68   *Peckingham Street, 1967.*

21   22   23

69   *The shop of Joseph Williams, fishmonger, Peckingham Street, c.1900.*

70   *Wilfred and Matilda Dancer preparing to leave their old shop on the corner of Peckingham Street and Hagley Street, 1967.*

Josiah Gaunt, surgeon, of Church Steps House, to Benjamin Partridge. Another well known owner was John Skidmore, who died in 1827. Early photographs of the corner of Peckingham Street and Hagley Street show a row of dilapidated cottages; these were purchased in the 1880s by John Dancer, a shoemaker and local Methodist preacher. He demolished the cottages and replaced them with a handsome three-storey block of shops with a large date stone 'JD 1890' on the corner.

John Dancer did not occupy the whole of the new block of shops; number 22 Peckingham Street was leased to George Mason, grocer; 23 Peckingham Street was occupied by Benjamin Thompson, hatter. John Dancer's boot and shoe shop was numbered 1 Hagley Street, with its entrance on the corner of Peckingham Street. He later leased these premises to Stephen Hilton & Sons. Edith Hall, milliner, occupied number 2 Hagley Street and Benjamin Law, cycle dealer, number 3. Dancers eventually occupied 23 Peckingham Street and all the shops on the Hagley Street side. When the shops were rebuilt in 1967, Dancers moved temporarily to the former Co-operative drapery store on the corner of Birmingham Street, but they soon returned to the new building which they still occupy.

Chapter IV

PUBS AND PUBLICANS

❧❧

The earliest court rolls of the manor of Halesowen record fines for the brewing of ale contrary to the assize. These may have been for brewing their beer too weak, giving short measure, or selling their beer too cheaply. In 1270, the following individuals were fined for such misdemeanours: Radolphus de Grene, Thomas de Linaker, Robertus Sumoner, Ricardus de Volatu, Christina de Coventre, Thomas Collings, John le Per de Oldbure, Johannes Simond, Philip Belegambe, Ricardus de Cackemor, Galfridus de Wesley, Hugo de Lowe, Jurdan de Cakemor, Adam Carpenter, Thomas de Puttewei and Ricardus de la Hethe. These names and those of other local brewers appear so regularly that the fines were evidently an early form of licensing. Indeed, there are so many brewers that most farmers living in the town or beside the main roads passing through the various hamlets must have sold beer to supplement their income.

The rental of Halesowen Abbey in 1500 records two inns, one in the borough of Halesowen, leased to John Hill for four nobles (£1 6s. 8d.) per year, and the other at St Kenelm's, where the inn, three closes of land and the 'Walshefeld' were leased to Hugh Westwood for £5 per year.[1] It is a reasonable assumption that John Hill kept the inn in High Street, which, after the sale of the manor to John Lyttelton in 1558, became known as the *Lyttelton Arms*. Hugh Westwood would have lived at the *Red Cow*, the farm house near St Kenelm's Church, Romsley, which was sold to the tenant Richard Harris in 1558.[2]

The Lyttelton Arms

Halesowen's premier inn and the venue for most public meetings and property auctions until the mid-19th century was the *Lyttelton Arms*. It is first mentioned in the deeds of neighbouring properties in 1648 as belonging to Sir Thomas Lyttelton and occupied by Isabel Weston, widow. The next occupant was Richard Heacock who paid for three chimneys in the hearth tax returns of 1672. He was followed by Alice Weston, widow, in 1686 and by Edward Hare in 1691.[3] No 18th-century publicans have been identified, although Aris's *Birmingham Gazette* carries an advertisement in 1746, placed by 'Top Dick', an innkeeper moving from *The Golden Cross* in Peckingham Street to the *Lyttelton Arms*, which he claimed was the most convenient house with the best stabling in Halesowen. Most of the Acts of Parliament

Halesowen Alehouse Recognizances 1755[4]

Licensee	Sureties	Licensee	Sureties
Roger Hornblow	John Sawyer	Samuel Nurey	George Bury
John Sawyer	Daniel Burton		William Hodgkins
John Palmer	John Hodgetts	Elizabeth Hodgetts	John Hodgetts
	Abraham Hodgetts		Abraham Hodgetts
George Hickins	William Partridge	Jane Clay	William Powell
	Daniel Burton		Josiah Powell
William Reade	John Hipkiss	Thomas Ellcock	William Powell
	Samuel Osborne		Clement Acton
Elizabeth Hale	Richard Hale	William Taylor	Clement Acton
John Osborne	John Dixon		William Powell
John Dixon	John Osborne	William Parkes	William Betterton
Jonathan Cox	Jacob Hall		William Brettell
John Stokes	John Shelburn	Hannah Taylor	Charles Booton
	Samuel Burton	William Betterton	Thomas Brettell
Mary Field	William Powell	Thomas Brettell	John Hipkiss
	George Bury	Joseph Millward	George Taylor
George Bury	William Powell		Walter Wood
Joseph Read	Charles Booton	Samuel Coley	William Millward
	John Millward		Walter Woodcock
Joseph Bromage	George Adams	Charles Millward	Josiah Green
	William Lovell		William Millward
Thomas Ingley	Thomas Smart	Abraham Johnson	Josiah Green
	James Cleft	John Hall	William Connop
William Wright	Clement Acton		Joseph Guest
	William Wright	Josiah Powell	William Powell

which give local turnpike trustees the power to improve local roads mention the *Lyttelton Arms* as the place for the trustees' meetings. It is an irony, therefore, that it was the diversion of the Dudley to Bromsgrove Road away from the High Street in 1773 which began the decline in fortune of Halesowen's oldest inn. The last innkeepers at the *Lyttelton Arms* were Charles Granger, in 1822, and Samuel Challoner, the tenant from 1830 until the closure of the inn in 1845. The building seen in old photographs of the High Street with the inn-sign of the *Old Lyttelton Arms* was in fact a private house built on the site of the old inn in 1845, which was later converted into a greengrocer's shop; a beerhouse licence was also obtained.

71 *The* Old Lyttelton Arms, *High Street, c.1920.*

The Crown Inn

One of the earliest mentions of a Halesowen inn by name is in the 1584 conveyance of *The Crown Inn*, situated in the borough of Halesowen, from Kenelm Hidley, felt maker of the parish of St Mary Magdalen, Bermondsey, to John Theker, mercer of Halesowen.[5] The inn, along with two acres of land in Huntingtree Field, two acres in High Field and half an acre in New Field, was in the occupation of Thomas Darby. In 1651, the property was conveyed by John Wight the elder, tanner, to Thomas Haden of Halesowen, yeoman, on the marriage of Wight's daughter Ann to Thomas Haden the younger of Rowley Regis.[6] By 1755, *The Crown Inn* was in the occupation of John Richards who was followed by William Connop and, in 1782, by William Stokes. The Stokes family then held *The Crown Inn* until 1851, when William Stokes is described as a victualler and cooper. Stokes probably

72 The Crown Inn, *Bull Ring, 1962, when occupied by a solicitor's office.*

conducted his cooper's business on the land opposite the inn, for when this plot was purchased by William Hayes for a garden to Comberton House, Great Cornbow, it was described as a garden that had formerly been a cooper's yard. Subsequent licensees of *The Crown Inn* were Mary Beach, James Haynes, William Butler, Elizabeth Humphries, Mary Whitcomb, Frank Norris, William George Green, Phillip Southall and Harry Smith. *The Crown Inn* closed in 1938 and was then used as offices by the solicitor, and one-time Mayor of Halesowen, Alfred George Rudge. The building was demolished in 1962.

The Plume of Feathers

Few Halesowen publicans made a living exclusively from the sale of beer and spirits. The occupants of the *Plume of Feathers* in Church Street were at various times maltsters and gun-barrel borers. This inn stood next to the Church House (rebuilt in 1897), and near the gate to the churchyard. The earliest recorded occupant, in 1756, was John Hipkiss, but in 1769 the licence was taken over by Joseph Harris, victualler and maltster. In his will of 1803, Joseph Harris left his real estate in the borough of Halesowen in his own occupation and all his stock of ale, malt, hops and liquors to his wife Ann. His connection with the local button factory is confirmed by the reference in his will to a debt of £100 owing from his son Joseph Harris and a further sum of £100 from his son and George Hinchliffe, his partner in trade, 'which I lent them to assist in carrying on their horn button trade'. By 1822, the *Plume of Feathers Inn* belonged to Aaron Rose, who was in partnership with Thomas Edge in the gun-barrel boring business at the former Halesowen Slitting Mill. Even as the gun-barrel business grew to employ 17 people, including several of his sons, Aaron Rose kept the licence of the pub into the 1850s. Later licensees were John Middleton, William Letts, and Moses Rose, who ran the *Plume of Feathers* until its closure in about 1890. The former inn was later rebuilt as three shops, called Church Street Chambers, which are still standing.

73   *Church Street, 1905, showing the former* Plume of Feathers Inn *behind the cyclist near to the churchyard gates.*

The most complete list of Halesowen inns is in the 1822 Shropshire Alehouse Recognizances.[7] It should be noted that this list excludes Cradley, Lutley and Warley Salop, which were in Worcestershire.

Halesowen Alehouse Recognizances 1822

Inn	Licensee	Sureties
Halesowen		
Bird in Hand	John Childs	Abraham Canadine, Halesowen, victualler
Bull's Head	Richard Turnley	Abraham Taylor, Halesowen, shopkeeper
Cock	Richard Eggington	Charles Tomlins, Halesowen, victualler
Crown	Mary Stokes	Abraham Canadine, Halesowen, victualler
Dog & Duck	William Grove	Henry Grove, Halesowen, brick maker
George	George Fitter	John Bissell, Halesowen, maltster
Golden Cross	Richard Russell	Richard Eggington, Halesowen, victualler
Half Moon	Charles Tomlins	Richard Eggington, Halesowen, victualler

Leopard	Catherine Day	Reuben Parsons, Halesowen, victualler
Lyttelton Arms	Charles Granger	Henry Round, Halesowen, glazier
Malt Shovel	Joseph Forrest	William Ganner, Halesowen, victualler
New Inn	Sarah Birch	William Jones, Halesowen, victualler
Plume of Feathers	Aaron Rose	John Bridge, Halesowen, victualler
Queen's Head	William Ganner	Joseph Forrest
Union Tavern, Islington	Mary Grove	Edward Grove, Halesowen, bricklayer

Hawne

Loyal Lodge at the Furnace	Reuben Parsons	Aaron Rose, Halesowen, victualler

Hill

Black Boy at the Quinton	Isaac Chambers	Daniel Parsons, Rowley Regis, shopkeeper
Holly Bush, Long Lane	Joseph Taylor	William Beesom, Halesowen, victualler
Swan, Long Lane	Thomas Cooper	Thomas Slinn, Halesowen, victualler

Hunnington

Malt Shovel	John Potter	Charles Granger, Halesowen, victualler
Sun	Hannah Turnley	John Childs, Halesowen, victualler

Lapal

Crown, Moor Street	Joseph Cooper	James Cooper, Halesowen, victualler

Ridgacre

Beech Tree, Beech Lane	John Bridge	Aaron Rose, Halesowen, victualler
Holly Bush, Red Hill	Elizabeth Hall	Reuben Parsons, Halesowen, victualler
Red Lion, Perry Hill	James Cooper	Joseph Cooper, Halesowen, victualler
Talbot, Beech Lane	William Beesom	John Bridge, Halesowen, victualler

Warley Salop

Cock & Magpie, Beech Lane	Edward Stedman	John Felton, Halesowen, victualler
George	Thomas Hurley	David Taylor, Halesowen, victualler
Pheasant, Warley Green	John Felton	Edward Stedman

Oldbury

Anchor	James Potter	John Cheshire, Halesowen, victualler
Bell	Ann Taylor	Edward Taylor, Oldbury, victualler
		Joseph Downing, Cradley Heath, roller of iron
Bird in Hand	Ann Crowley	Joseph Downing, Cradley Heath, roller of iron
Blue Anchor	Charles Hodgkins	John White, Halesowen, victualler
Boat	William Fisher	John White, Halesowen, victualler
Brown Lion	Joseph Smith	Joseph Simpson, Halesowen, victualler
Bull's Head	John Cheshire	James Potter, Halesowen, victualler
Cart & Horses	Thomas Collins	Thomas Standley, Halesowen, victualler
Collier	Thomas Slinn	Thomas Cooper, Long Lane, victualler
Cross	Joseph Slinn	Thomas Cooper, Halesowen, victualler
Flower Pot	Joseph Green	Thomas Round, Halesowen, victualler

Gate	Joseph Underhill	Benjamin Hurley, Halesowen, victualler
Gate	Benjamin Hurley	Thomas Hurley, Halesowen, victualler
George & Dragon	Joseph Sambrook	Samuel Parish, Halesowen, victualler
		James Hardman, borough of Halesowen, hinge maker
New Inn	Thomas Standley	Thomas Collins, Halesowen, victualler
Red Cow	Thomas Round	Joseph Green, Halesowen, victualler
Seven Stars	John White	William Fisher, Halesowen, victualler
Talbot	Samuel Parish	Joseph Brettell, Halesowen, victualler
Wagon & Horses	David Taylor	Thomas Hurley, Halesowen, victualler
Whimsy	Hannah Rowley	Joseph Brettell, Halesowen, victualler
White Horse	Joseph Brettell	Samuel Parish, Halesowen, victualler
White Lion	John Simpson	Joseph Smith, Halesowen, victualler

74   *The* New Inn, *Whitehall, built at the junction of two turnpike roads in the 1760s.*

Several Halesowen inns came into being as the result of alterations to the road pattern of the town. The *New Inn*, Whitehall, was built soon after 1762, when the newly turnpiked road from Colly Gate to Halesowen joined the existing Birmingham to Blakedown turnpike at what was to become known as the 'Finger Post'. The *New Inn* naturally attracted the coaching trade. Although it was not a coaching inn in the sense that it had an arrangement with stage coach proprietors to change horses, most of the stage coaches stopped here to collect and drop off local passengers. The licensee, William Taylor, did supply post horses for private coaches, and his house hosted many property auctions and official meetings. His widow, Betty Taylor, was still running the inn as late as 1822. The next licensee was Sarah Birch, but by 1839 the *New Inn* was owned by Charles Birch and occupied by George Granger.

The 1840 directory listed the following coach services as stopping at George Granger's *New Commercial Inn*, Whitehall:

> To Birmingham—Independent, from the *New Inn*, daily, leaves 1/4 before 10 am, returns 7 pm.
>
> To Birmingham—Favourite, from the *New Inn*, daily, leaves 1/4 before 10 am, returns 1/4 before 6 pm.
>
> To Kidderminster & Stourport—Favourite, from the *New Inn*, daily, leaves 1/4 before 6 pm. Returns 1/4 before 10 am

75 *The* Shenstone
Hotel *was built soon
after the construction of
Bromsgrove Street in
the 1850s. It is seen
here about 1905 when
the licensee was George
Arm.*

To Stourbridge—Erin-go-Bragh, from the *New Inn*, daily, leaves 10 am., returns 1/4 before
    6 pm.
To Stourbridge—Independent, from the *New Inn*, daily, leaves 7 pm., returns 1/4 before
    10 am.

The cessation of the Birmingham to Stourbridge coach in 1850, and the opening
of a new route for the Dudley to Bromsgrove turnpike road along Bromsgrove
Street in 1855, marked the end of the *New Inn*'s supremacy in Halesowen. Even
the Justices of the Peace ceased to meet there after the opening in the 1860s of
the Public Offices in Great Cornbow. At least the lunch to celebrate the opening
of the new railway line to Halesowen in March 1878 was held at the *New Inn*.
The licensee in 1881, Giles Melley, described himself as a grocer and innkeeper,
suggesting that he had had to diversify to stay in business. Later occupants of the
New Inn were John Roberts and Frederick Williams. The *New Inn* closed in 1955
and was rebuilt as offices by Eric Charles Emery in about 1960.

The *Shenstone Hotel* was built on the corner of Birmingham Road and the
newly opened Bromsgrove Street about 1855. The first licensee was Moses Rose,
whose family kept the *Plume of Feathers* in Church Street and leased the gun barrel
mill on the other side of Bromsgrove Street. In 1860, Felix Briggs Granger was
the occupant; he described his house as the *Shenstone Commercial Hotel*, Posting
House & Inland Revenue Office, Birmingham Road, evidently seeing the hotel
as a successor to the Granger family's *New Inn*. A later licensee, George Pearsall,
called himself a 'hotel keeper' and invested in an advertisement in the 1876 *Post
Office Directory of Worcestershire*. His publicity was successful, for the celebration lunch
to mark the opening of the Halesowen Railway extension to Rubery in October
1883 was held at the *Shenstone Hotel*. Subsequent occupants, such as Harriett Jones,
Edward Beirne and George Arm, maintained the sign as the *Shenstone Hotel*, but
later licensees like John Hill and John Allen accepted that the Shenstone was an
ordinary public house.

76   *Architect's drawing of the* Golden Cross Inn, *1911.*

The Golden Cross

In a period when the Salvation Army, the temperance movement and even the Methodists saw drink as one of the chief evils of the day, it was not surprising that the Halesowen Justices resolved in 1906, 'That in the opinion of the Justices … there are too many licences in proportion to the population, and that steps be taken under the Licensing Act of 1904 to reduce them'. It was further resolved at a later meeting that the *Star & Garter Inn*, Birmingham Street, the *Leopard Inn*, Church Street, and *The Golden Cross Inn*, Peckingham Street, were not needed.

The Golden Cross Inn on Peckingham Street was a peculiar choice for closure as it was an ancient inn, with good stabling behind. It is first mentioned by name in a 1746 advert placed by the aforementioned 'Top Dick', who 'is removed from *The Golden Cross* to the *Lyttelton's Arms*'. *The Golden Cross* was a wide two-storey building with three small dormer windows lighting the attics. Its extensive stable yard was entered from Birmingham Road, the new street constructed by the Trustees of the Birmingham to Blakedown Turnpike Road over the old Laconstone Brook. It must have been a respectable house, as the turnpike trustees occasionally held their meetings there. The inn was owned from the early 18th century by Joshua Male, then by Joseph Male and his son Joseph. In 1815, it passed to Thomas Bate of Hagley on his marriage to Susannah Male.[8] Tenants of *The Golden Cross* included, from 1810 to 1906, John Wakefield, Richard Russell, Thomas Parish, William Bond, Ralph Kent, Thomas White, John White, Joseph Nock, William Ware and Moses Willetts. *The Golden Cross* may have been a candidate for closure in 1906 because of the recent death of the owner, Joseph Nock, and the sale of his various business properties.[9] The *Leopard* also closed at this time, but the *Star and Garter* survived another 60 years and was not demolished until 1969.

77 *The* Star and Garter, *Birmingham Street, 1955.*

78 *The former* Malt Shovel Inn, *Church Street, 1965. There was a malting between Church Street and New Road, but none of the recorded occupants of the* Malt Shovel *was in the malting business.*

Maltings

With two large maltings in Great Cornbow, four in Hagley Street, one in High Street, and another in Church Street, there was a sufficient surplus of malt produced in 19th-century Halesowen to have supplied a large brewery. None of the maltsters, however, developed their businesses in this way or attempted to buy up licensed premises until about 1884, when Joseph Cooper occupied a malting or brewery behind Church Street. From 1904, these premises appear in directories as Carr &

79 *The* Fox Inn, *Great Cornbow, when owned by Joseph Cooper. The building has now been converted into offices.*

Co.'s Halesowen Brewery. Joseph Cooper lived at the Limes, Grammar School Lane. Although he at one time owned the *Globe Inn*, Peckingham Street and the *Fox Inn*, Great Cornbow, he failed to build a chain of licensed premises sufficient to make the brewery viable.

In the absence of a significant brewery in Halesowen, licensed premises in the town were gradually bought up by the big breweries.

Public houses owned by breweries in 1951[10]

Ansells
Black Horse Inn, Illey Lane
Forge Inn, Dudley Road, Halesowen
Hawne Tavern, Attwood Street, Hawne
Loyal Lodge Inn, Furnace Hill,, Hawne
Rose and Crown Inn, Hasbury
Rose and Crown Inn, High Street, Cradley
Why Not Inn, Stocking Street, Cradley

Atkinson's
Fox Inn, Cornbow, Halesowen

Marmaduke Valentine Beard
Old Lyttelton Arms Inn, High Street, Halesowen

Bull's Head Ltd, 43 Cannon Street, Birmingham
Fox Hunt Inn, Hayley Green, Halesowen

W. Butler & Co. Ltd, Birmingham.
Horse and Jockey Inn, Mogul Lane, Cradley

Daniel Batham & Sons, Delph Brewery, Brierley Hill
White Horse Inn, High Street, Cradley

A.H. Cook, Lye
Park Lane Tavern, Park Lane, Cradley

Darby's
Talbot Inn, Colley Gate, Cradley
Travellers' Rest Inn, Long Lane, Hill and
  Cakemore
Vine Inn, Two Gates, Cradley

Dares'
Hare and Hounds Inn, Hasbury
Old Royal Inn, Islington
Plough Hotel, Rumbow
Whitley Inn, Stourbridge Road,
  Halesowen

Davenport's
Queen's Head Inn, Birmingham Street,
  Halesowen

Thomas Hartshorne, Netherton
Star Inn, Cornbow, Halesowen

Ind Coope & Allsopp
Black Horse Inn, Manor Lane, Lapal
British Arms Inn, New Street, Halesowen
Holly Bush Inn, High Street, Cradley
King Edward VII Inn, Stourbridge Road,
  Halesowen
Red Lion Inn, Hagley Road, Halesowen
Townsend Stores, Church Street,
  Halesowen

John Joule & Son Ltd, Stone, Staffs
Anchor Inn, Gorsty Hill, Halesowen

Mitchells and Butlers
Acorn Inn, Malt Mill Lane, Hill and
  Cakemore
Crown Inn, Moor Street, Lapal
George Hotel, Church Street, Halesowen
Lyttelton Arms Inn, High Street,
  Halesowen
New Inn, Whitehall Road, Halesowen
Royal Oak Inn, Carters Lane, Lapal
Shenstone Hotel, Whitehall Road,
  Halesowen
Stag and Three Horse Shoes Inn, Halesowen
  Road, Quinton
Swan Inn, Long Lane, Hill and
  Cakemore
Vine Inn, Lyde Green, Cradley

Wagon and Horses Inn, Stourbridge Road,
  Halesowen

People's Refreshment Houses Assn. Ltd
County Inn, The Nimmings, Cakemore

Frederick Smith
British Arms Inn, Furlong Lane, Cradley
Bull's Head Inn, Hagley Street,
  Halesowen
Crown Inn, Lyde Green, Cradley
Nelson Inn, Spring Hill, Halesowen
Railway Inn, Mucklow Hill, Halesowen
Samson and Lion Inn, Stourbridge Road,
  Halesowen

G.H. Stafford
Old White Lion Inn, Windmill Hill,
  Cradley

Benjamin Tromans
Duke William Inn, Furlong Lane,
  Cradley

Truman Hanbury & Co., Burton.
Old Crown Inn, High Town, Cradley

Twists
Shelton Inn, Belle Vale, Halesowen

Wolverhampton & Dudley
Ashley Hotel, Long Lane, Hill and
  Cakemore
Beehive Inn, Spring Hill, Hasbury
Black Horse Inn, Banners Lane, Cradley
Blue Ball, Blue Ball Lane, Cradley
Bridge Inn, Bridge Street, Cradley
Bull's Head Inn, Overend, Cradley
Crown Inn, Barrack Lane, Cradley
Fairfield, Fairfield Road, Hill and
  Cakemore
Maypole Inn, Maypole Hill, Cradley
Round of Beef Inn, Windmill Hill,
  Cradley
Victoria Inn, Malt Mill Lane, Hill and
  Cakemore
Vine Inn, Cornbow, Halesowen
Wagon and Horses, Long Lane, Hill and
  Cakemore

Chapter V

ROADS, CANALS AND RAILWAYS

⌘⌘

Turnpike Roads

During the early 18th century, the English main road network was dramatically improved as a result of hundreds of Acts of Parliament, which empowered groups of local gentry and tradesmen to charge travellers using the main roads passing through their districts. The income from tolls was used to improve the road surface and to make useful diversions. Such roads were called 'turnpikes' after the style of gate erected at the toll houses, which featured upturned pikes along the top rail. Three major Turnpike Acts of 1727, 1753 and 1762 kept Halesowen at the forefront of this movement to promote trade by improving the quality of the nation's roads.

The Bromsgrove to Dudley Turnpike

The ancient road which ran from Dudley through Halesowen to Bromsgrove was turnpiked in 1727, under 'An Act for repairing the Roads leading from the Town of Bromsgrove to the Town of Dudley in the County of Worcester; and from the said Town of Bromsgrove to the Town of Birmingham in the County of Warwick'. The original route of this road entered the parish at Gorsty Hill, dropped down to a bridge over the Stour at Furnace, and then climbed Furnace Hill to enter the town via Church Street. Its route continued up Peckingham Street and left the town via another bridge over the Stour at Cornbow. The road then passed through Hunnington, over Romsley Hill, and met the Birmingham to Bromsgrove road, turnpiked under the same Act, at Lydiate Ash. Among the trustees of the 1727 Act were Sir Thomas Lyttelton of Hagley Hall, William Lea of the Grange, Thomas Wight of Halesowen and Henry Haden of Haden Hill.

Each Turnpike Act gave the trustees the power to raise tolls and repair the roads for 21 years only. At the end of this term, the trustees had to go back to Parliament and obtain a new Act to continue their powers. There were further Acts passed that covered the Bromsgrove to Dudley road in 1742, 1773, 1794, 1816 and 1854. Each new Act gave the trustees the opportunity to raise the tolls, put up new toll houses, or to divert the road. The Act of 1773 permitted the trustees to realign the road so as to avoid the steep gradients at Gorsty Hill, Furnace Hill and Romsley Hill. The main result of this was a diversion of the road at the bottom of Gorsty

80 *The former toll collector's house at Grange Hill on the Bromsgrove to Dudley Turnpike, 1966.*

Hill, which directed traffic south-east along Forge Lane to meet the Birmingham to Hagley Turnpike east of the bridge at the bottom of Mucklow Hill. A public house called *The Bridge Inn* stood on Forge Lane just to the north of this junction; it was renamed *The Railway Inn* in the 1880s. The 1773 Act also led to a minor realignment of the road at Romsley, easing the gradient of Romsley Hill.

The 1794 Bromsgrove to Dudley Turnpike Act gave the trustees power to construct three-quarters of a mile of new road from the *Bush Inn*, Dudley to the Cinder Banks. No other diversions are specified in subsequent Bromsgrove to Dudley Turnpike Acts, but some time after the first edition Ordnance Survey map was surveyed (possibly as early as 1811, but not published until 1831) the old route over Gorsty Hill was abandoned in favour of a new road from Haden Cross to the bottom of Coombs Road. The new road became known as Haden Hill Road and a turnpike toll collector's house was built at its junction with Furnace Lane. A further diversion took the road west of the forge, to a new junction with the Birmingham to Hagley Road, west of the bridge at the bottom of Mucklow Hill. This new section of road soon became known as Dudley Road. It was not until the last Bromsgrove to Dudley Turnpike Act was passed in 1854 that this line of road was continued from its junction with Mucklow Hill, alongside Halesowen Mill, to join the old line of the turnpike near the Grange. This new road became known as Bromsgrove Street. A new hotel called *The Shenstone* was built on the corner of Bromsgrove Street and Whitehall, and a public house named *The Woodman* was built at the other end of the new road. Henceforth, travellers and hauliers using the Bromsgrove to Dudley turnpike bypassed Halesowen town centre altogether. The Bromsgrove to Dudley road continued to be repaired by the turnpike trustees until the last Act of Parliament for the road expired in 1876.

81 *Former toll collector's house at Hayley Green on the Birmingham to Blakedown turnpike, c.1910.*

The Birmingham to Hagley Turnpike

A 1727 Act of Parliament to improve the road from Birmingham to Stourbridge applied only to the route via Dudley and was of no benefit to Halesowen. It wasn't until 1753 that the road from Birmingham to Halesowen was turnpiked. In April of that year William Shenstone, writing from the Leasowes, Halesowen, to his friend, Lady Luxborough, said that he had drawn up a 'copy of a petition to Sir George about the Turnpike'.[1] He was referring to the Bill before Parliament to improve several roads leading from the Market House in Stourbridge. The subsequent Act of 1753 turnpiked the road from Birmingham, through Halesowen, to Blakedown Pool in the parish of Hagley, and the road from Stourbridge to Bromsgrove, which crossed the Birmingham to Blakedown road at Hagley. William Shenstone and Sir George Lyttelton of Hagley Hall were among the original trustees of these turnpike roads.

The Birmingham to Hagley turnpike road used to enter Halesowen via Whitehall, Rumbow and Birmingham Street, where there were several inns including, on the west side, the *Queen's Head* and the *Red Lion*, and on the east side, the *Cross Guns*, the *Royal Oak* and the *Star and Garter*. Some time before 1780, the Birmingham to Hagley Trustees chose to divert the road at Rumbow and build a new section of road over the Laconstone Brook to enter the High Street at its junction with Peckingham Street. The new section became known as Birmingham Road and that part of the High Street from Peckingham Street to Grange Mill Lane (later called Laurel Lane) became known as Hagley Street.

82   *The* Railway Inn, *Forge Lane, c.1960.*

Another realignment took place near the dangerous crossing of the River Stour at the bottom of Mucklow Hill. As early as 1679, Thomas Wight of Halesowen, felt maker, had given evidence to an inquiry that the Maltmill Bridge, in the roadway from Halesowen towards Birmingham, was 'out of repair and dangerous for passengers for that this deponent having occasion to come over the said bridge called Maltmill Bridge … slipped into a hole therein and broke his arm'. In a 1748 conveyance of ¾ acre of land called the Mill Close, one of the boundaries was a 'roadway leading from the mill towards the bridge called Broken Bridge'.[2] At a meeting of the trustees of the Birmingham to Hagley Turnpike in July 1792, it was ordered that the committee appointed to direct the improvements between the 5th milestone from Birmingham to Hagley Lane Turnpike Gate, 'do immediately widen and improve the bridge below Whitehall over the water running from Mr Ward's mill so as to raise the valley of the road there'.[3] By 1802, the bridge had been replaced and the road realigned. That year the trustees ordered that Thomas Connop, whose family had a beerhouse near the bridge, should 'have the old road and shred of land near the bridge at Halesowen adjoining his land and divided by the mill pool at the sum of seven guineas'. The Connup family continued to hold the *Bridge Inn* until the 1880s. Their successors renamed it the *Railway Inn* due to its proximity to the railway station, which opened in 1878.

The 1818 Birmingham to Hagley Turnpike Act gave the trustees the power to alter

> the present line of the road from the meeting house at a place called the Quinton in the parish of Halesowen in the county of Salop for the distance of 600 yards or thereabouts in a straight line … to a place called Crock Street in the same parish … Part of the said road from the said meeting house to the *Black Boy* aforesaid will be unnecessary to the continued turnpike.

The *Black Boy* was an ancient public house on the road to Birmingham which closed soon after it was bypassed by the new line of road. The 1841 Birmingham to Hagley Turnpike Act sanctioned another alteration to the line of the road at Spring Hill as the road left Halesowen. A Birmingham to Hagley Turnpike toll-collector's house survived at the corner of College Road, Quinton until the 1930s. Another toll-collector's house stood west of the junction of Lutley Lane, Hayley Green.

The Stourbridge to Halesowen Turnpikes

Improvements to the road to Stourbridge were made following an Act of Parliament of 1762, appointing trustees to turnpike the roads from Stourbridge to Colly Gate and from Colly Gate to Halesowen. A toll collector's house still stands on the corner of Stourbridge Road and Attwood Street. A further Act of 1782 gave the trustees powers to build a new section of road from the termination of the Stourbridge Turnpike Road at Townsend, over the Earls Brook to connect with the Birmingham Turnpike Road between the lower end of Dog Lane (now Church Lane) and a newly erected public house called the *New Inn*. This created the junction known thereafter as the Finger Post and made the nearby *New Inn* the principal coaching hotel in Halesowen. The original 1762 Stourbridge to Colly Gate Act also turnpiked the road from Dudley to Northfield, which passed east of Halesowen, via Long Lane and Carters Lane. These two ancient lanes were not directly connected until Kent Road was built in the 1930s.

83 *Former toll collector's house at Short Cross on the Colley Gate to Halesowen turnpike, 1973.*

With the expiration of the last Turnpike Acts in the 1870s, the turnpike trustees sold off their assets, closed their accounts and gave any surplus to the surveyors of highways of the parishes through which their roads passed. In April 1876, the trustees of the Bromsgrove to Dudley Turnpike sold the toll house at the top of Grange Hill to Ferdinando Dudley Lea Smith of the Grange for £80. In November of the same year, they sold the site of the former toll house near the Furnace to Joseph Sidaway of Coombs for £35. The responsibility for maintaining the roads through Halesowen theoretically fell back upon the parish. In reality, little would be done to repair the roads until the creation of Worcestershire County Council in 1889, with a mandate to maintain all main roads in the county.

The Dudley Canal

The records of the Stourbridge ironmaster, Thomas Foley, show that he maintained a large iron warehouse at Bewdley on the River Severn. The local road network was totally unsuitable for the chains of heavily-laden packhorses which conveyed the products of Hales Furnace, and his other Stour Valley forges and furnaces, to this warehouse. He must, therefore, have supported the Act of Parliament of 1662 which authorised works on the River Stour to make it navigable from the ironworks and collieries near Stourbridge to the River Severn. Although the engineer, Andrew Yarranton, completed some of the necessary locks between Stourbridge and Kidderminster, the project failed for want of funds. No viable scheme for making the Stour navigable emerged until the Staffordshire and Worcestershire Canal Act of 1766 authorised the construction of the 46-mile Staffordshire and Worcestershire Canal, from the Trent and Mersey Canal at Great Haywood, near Stafford, through Wolverhampton and down the Stour Valley to Bewdley. Bewdley rejected the scheme, but the site chosen by the canal company for its wharfs on the River Severn was to create the prosperous new town of Stourport. The canal opened in 1771, providing a new outlet for the products of the Staffordshire coalfields and the Black Country.

In 1776, the Stourbridge Canal Act authorised a three-mile branch from the Staffordshire and Worcestershire Canal at Stourton into the town of Stourbridge. The leading shareholder was Lord Dudley. Another Act of 1776, also promoted by Lord Dudley, led to the construction of the Dudley Canal, running from Black Delph, on the Stourbridge Canal, to Parkhead, near Dudley. A second Dudley Canal Act in 1785 authorised the extension of the Dudley Canal to Tipton through a 3,172-yard tunnel under the town of Dudley. It was the third Dudley Canal Act of 1793 that authorised the 11-mile canal through Halesowen connecting with the Worcester and Birmingham Canal at Selly Oak. The Dudley No.2 Canal, as it became known, included the 557-yard Gorsty Hill Tunnel, the huge earth embankment at the Leasowes, and the 3,795-yard Lapal Tunnel, which took boats four hours to pass through. The canal opened in 1797.

The Dudley Canal Company opened a wharf south-west of the bridge, taking Mucklow Hill over the canal.[4] This became known as Haywood Wharf. The first

84   *Hawne Basin, Dudley Canal, 1974.*

Superintendent was Thomas Brettell, but in 1812 the Canal Company appointed Thomas Brewin to the post at a salary of £250 per year, which increased to £300 in 1819 and to £400 in 1839. Brewin was a major shareholder in the Canal Company and lived at the fine three-storey house on the wharf, now called Haywood House and used as offices by Walter Somers Ltd. In 1833, the Dudley Canal Company agreed to build a bathroom onto the house if Brewin paid for the fittings. Brewin also owned Hawne Bank Farm, probably purchased as an investment in the coal underneath the farmland. Thomas Brewin died in 1854, by which time the Dudley No.1 and No.2 Canals had been amalgamated with the Birmingham Canal Navigations.

The Dudley Canal was first exploited by colliery owners such as the Attwoods of Hawne, who built a tramway from their Old Hawne Colliery, over the Bromsgrove to Dudley turnpike road, to a canal basin near Mucklow Hill. The basin became known as Hawne Basin. In 1828, Joseph Darby of Greenhill, nail ironmonger, bought a plot of land near Hawne Basin for his new nail warehouse. This was later purchased by Walter Somers for his first forge. Abraham

85   *Former canal agent's house, Mucklow Hill, 1974.*

86 *The entrance to the disused Lapal Tunnel after the wall was struck by lightning in 1928.*

Barnsley started an ironworks by the canal at Coombs Wood in 1860. This was to develop into the huge Stewarts & Lloyds tube works. Thomas Bissell of Webb's Green built another nail warehouse where the canal crossed Manor Lane, and John Samuel Dawes of Lapal Lodge opened the Manor Lane Colliery in 1864, sending the coal by barge through the Lapal Tunnel to Birmingham.

The building of the new Netherton tunnel in 1858, with its twin towpaths, gave carriers an alternative route to Birmingham, leaving the Dudley No.2 Canal as something of a backwater. The Canal Company kept only a wharfinger or toll collector at Haywood Wharf. The wharfingers included William Grove, Charles Brindley, Hiram Beazley and Mary Beard, who was still in the post in 1940. The Lapal Tunnel closed after a roof fall in 1917, and the last commercial boat to use the canal took steel tubes from Stewarts & Lloyds in 1969. The canal was cut by the widening of Mucklow Hill and Manor Lane in the 1960s. Hawne Basin is now a busy marina, full of pleasure boats, but there is little trace of the canal between Manor Lane and the mouth of Lapal Tunnel.

Railways

It is surprising that a rapidly expanding industrial town the size of Halesowen was not connected to the railway network until 1878. The Oxford, Worcester and Wolverhampton Railway (later known as the West Midland Railway) completed the section of the line between Stourbridge and Dudley in 1852. An Act of 1860 authorised the Stourbridge Railway to construct a branch from the West Midland Railway at Stourbridge, through Cradley Heath to Old Hill, linking up with the London and North Western Railway at Galton Junction, and the Great Western Railway at Handsworth. The new line was run by the G.W.R., and the station at Cradley Heath opened in April 1863. This gave a boost to the economy of Cradley, which was still part of Halesowen, but already an industrial town in its own right. The Stourbridge Railway was extended to Old Hill in January 1866,

87 Halesowen Railway Station, 1959.

and through-services from Stourbridge to Snow Hill Station, Birmingham, started in 1867. In the meantime, the West Midland Railway had secured an 1862 Act of Parliament to construct a branch from Dudley to Halesowen, which had to cross the Stourbridge Railway at Old Hill. The route also involved making a tunnel under Haden Hill. The West Midland Railway was taken over in 1863 by the G.W.R., which was less keen on the Halesowen branch and let the powers in the 1862 Act expire. New powers were obtained in the Great Western Railway Act of 1872, but the line, when built, did not go straight through to Dudley. The lines from Halesowen and Dudley both turned east before joining the Stourbridge to Birmingham line at Old Hill. Through-passengers had to get out and change platforms. Both lines opened on 1 March 1878, with ten trains daily from Old Hill to Halesowen; there was a marked increase in the number of people going to Dudley market, which was unwelcome news for Halesowen shopkeepers.

The railway south of Halesowen was constructed by a different company altogether. An Act was passed in 1865 authorising the Halesowen and Bromsgrove Branch Railways Company to construct a new line from the Midland Railway in the parish of Kings Norton to the township of Hill in the parish of Halesowen, where the G.W.R. already planned to terminate their line from Dudley. The Chairman and main shareholder was George William Lord Lyttelton, who owned most of the land through which the line would pass. The G.W.R. and the Midland Railway signed an agreement that year that, once the railway was built, the two companies would maintain and run the line jointly. The Halesowen and Bromsgrove Branch Railway found it difficult to raise money for the line and therefore to secure the services of a good contractor. Further Acts of Parliament in 1872 and 1876 gave the company more time to complete the line and allowed some deviations from the original route. The name of the company was changed to the Halesowen Railway, after which yet another Act was passed in 1879, giving them the power to use the newly opened G.W.R. station on Mucklow Hill rather than build their own station.

88 *Halesowen Railway Station, c.1900, showing Station Master Herbert Payton's garden.*

A feature of the line was the Dowery Dell Viaduct, which carried the line 100ft. above a stream, just south of Hunnington Station. The steel trestle viaduct was, however, subject to strict weight and speed restrictions. The line finally opened on 10 September 1883. The Halesowen Railway Company never paid a dividend to its shareholders and was wound up in 1906, the two operating companies agreeing to purchase the undertaking jointly, an arrangement sanctioned by the Midland Railway Act of 1906.

As Halesowen was a G.W.R. station, most of its passenger and goods traffic was run by that company. The bulk of the services south of Halesowen were operated by the Midland Railway, but the G.W.R. did exercise its right to run a few trains to Rubery. A short branch line from Halesowen Station up to the canal basin, serving Lloyd & Lloyd and Walter Somers works, was built by the G.W.R. in 1902. The Station Master, Herbert Payton, was justifiably proud of the

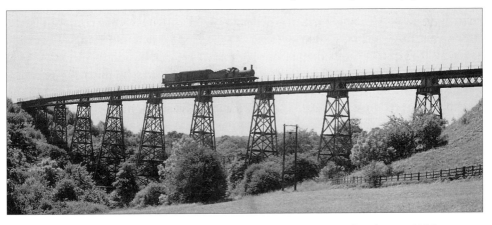

89 *Dowery Dell Viaduct on the line between Halesowen and Rubery, c.1920.*

90 *The last workmen's special train from Longbridge to Halesowen on 29 August 1958.*

gardens at Halesowen Station, which fitted in with the G.W.R. promotion of Halesowen as a commuter town adjacent to the beautiful countryside of north Worcestershire.

As early as 1913, the Birmingham and Midland Motor Omnibus Company (later the Midland Red) started a motor bus service from Halesowen to Birmingham. The Midland Railway passenger services between Halesowen and New Street were withdrawn during the 1914-18 war and never resumed, although the morning and evening trains through Halesowen to Longbridge, where the Austin Motor Company was expanding rapidly, continued. The G.W.R., however, maintained its passenger services to Halesowen for another 10 years. The transport of coal and heavy goods to Halesowen's industry had always been the prime concern of both companies, but this did not lessen the shock when, in 1927, the G.W.R. announced that passenger services from Old Hill to Halesowen were to be replaced by a bus service. There was, therefore, no passenger service provided by either company after 1927, other than the L.M.S. workmen's trains from Longbridge to New Street and the similar G.W.R. services from Longbridge to Old Hill. In the 1950s, car workers began to run their own cars, so the numbers using these trains dwindled. The workmen's trains were busy again during the fuel rationing brought about by the Suez crisis in 1956-7, but the last workmen's special, hauled by Western Region 0-6-0 pannier tank engine no.7430, ran from Longbridge to Old Hill on 29 August 1958. When Manor Lane was widened in 1959, a new railway bridge was built, suggesting that the line had some future. The London Midland Region, however, soon announced the withdrawal of its New Street to Longbridge trains. The last train ran from Longbridge on 1 January 1960, hauled by a British Railways Standard Class 4-6-0 No.73159.

Some goods trains continued on the line, serving Stewarts & Lloyds and Walter Somers, and bringing coal for the merchants at Halesowen, Hunnington and Rubery. There were also deliveries to and from the Blue Bird Toffee Factory at Hunnington. When the M5 Motorway was planned in the early 1960s, however, it was assumed that the railway from Halesowen to Rubery would be closed, and no provision was made for railway bridges. This section of the line was officially closed in January 1964. The track was lifted and the Dowery Dell Viaduct was taken down in April 1965. At Halesowen, the Coombs Wood Works stopped sending their tubes by rail in 1967 and goods services to Halesowen ceased on 9 September 1968; the track was lifted in 1969.

Chapter VI

Gentlemen's Houses

᷒ᝌᦾ

The Grange

The term 'grange' usually refers to a barn or farmstead distant from the centre of an estate, particularly one owned by the church or an abbey. Halesowen Abbey had several granges, such as Hell Grange and Farley Grange in Romsley, and Howley Grange in Lapal. The grange near Halesowen Abbey was probably the home farm of the manor of Halesowen. In 1558, it was leased for 1,000 years by Thomas Blount and George Tuckey to John Ive of Halesowen, yeoman, the sitting tenant, for £125, plus a token payment of 12d. per year. At this time it was described as 'all that their Mansion House situate and being near unto the Town of Halesowen aforesaid in the said County of Salop commonly called the Graunge with the appurtenances now in the tenure or occupation of the said John Ive'.[1] John Ive's daughter Joyce married William Lea of Halesowen, thus starting a long association between the Lea family and the Grange. Some idea of the size of the house can be gained from the Shropshire hearth tax returns of 1672, when Mr William Lea paid for five hearths.

In 1709 William Lea, son of John Lea of the Grange, married Frances Ward, sister of William Ward, 5th Lord Ward and 10th Lord Dudley. This proved a very advantageous marriage, for, in 1740, William Ward died without a direct heir. Whilst the barony of Ward and the castle and lands at Dudley passed to his cousin

and heir male, John Ward of Sedgeley, the barony of Dudley passed to his nephew and heir general, Ferdinando Dudley Lea, son of William and Frances Lea of the Grange. The title of Lord Dudley only

91 *The Grange, Halesowen, home of the Lea Smith family, c.1900.*

applied to the resident of the Grange for 17 years. When Ferdinando Dudley Lea, 11th Lord Dudley, died at the Grange in 1757, the barony of Dudley became extinct. John Ward 6th Lord Ward, on the other hand, received the new title of Viscount Dudley and Ward in 1763 and his descendants continued to hold that title and to develop the mineral rights on the Dudley estate.

The style of the east front of the Grange suggests that the house was rebuilt by Ferdinando Dudley Lea, Lord Dudley, about 1750, although the south side is of a later date. If this was the case then William Shenstone, who often mentions Lord Dudley in letters to his friends, would surely have remarked upon it. Shenstone was always upset if Lord Lyttelton called on Lord Dudley at the Grange without visiting the Leasowes as well. On the death of Ferdinando Dudley Lea, Lord Dudley in 1757, the Grange was left to the eldest surviving son of his sister, Ann Smith, who lived on at the Grange until 1762, calling herself (quite illegally) Baroness Dudley. It was probably her son William Smith, or his son Ferdinando Smith, who rebuilt the Grange, or at least made further alterations to the house, in the late 18th century. The Grange stayed in the Smith family until the death of Ferdinando Dudley Lea Smith in 1905; it later became the home of Seth Somers and was opened as the Somers' Sports and Social Club on 27 April 1951.

Hawne House

Humphrey Pearsall, like John Ive of the Grange, signed a 1,000-year lease of his land from Thomas Blount and George Tuckey in 1558.[2] The charities board in Halesowen Church records that John Pearsall of Hawne, in his will of 1644, gave £5 towards building a free school in Halesowen. He also gave 1s. to the poor of Hawne and 5s. to the poor of Hasbury and Halesowen, to be paid yearly, on St Thomas Day, for ever. Hawne House must have been a large establishment for, in 1672, Mr Tho. Pearcehall paid tax on five hearths at his house in Hawne. Various members of the Pearsall family appear on lists of churchwardens and feoffees of

92 *Hawne House in the 18th century.*

Halesowen Grammar School. In 1711 Thomas, son of Thomas Pearsall of Hawne, Salop, gentleman, matriculated at Trinity College, Oxford, aged seventeen. Mr Thomas Pearsall was listed as a trustee of the Bromsgrove to Dudley turnpike road in 1727. John, son of Thomas Pearsall of Halesowen, gentleman, matriculated at Pembroke College, Oxford, in 1736 aged eighteen.

Thomas Pearsall died in 1759 leaving Hawne House to his son, the Rev. John Pearsall, who was then headmaster of the Royal Grammar School in Guildford. The Guildford Corporation minutes of 1765 show, however, that there were no scholars attending the grammar school due to the 'intolerable negligence and misbehaviour of the master'.[3] In 1770, this same Rev. John Pearsall assumed the name of Sir John Peshall Bart, claiming descent from one John Peshall of Horseley, Staffordshire, who was made a baronet in 1612. He even went to the expense of altering the gravestone in Halesowen churchyard which recorded the death in 1714 of his grandfather, Thomas Pearsall, to read Peshall instead of Pearsall.

Following the death of the Rev. Pearsall in 1778, Hawne House was occupied by George Attwood, who had bought the nearby Corngreaves Iron Works, Rowley Regis, from the bankrupt Price Thomas of Corngreaves.[4] The Attwood family enterprises prospered, and George's son, James, built a fine house called Corngreaves Hall across the River Stour in Rowley parish. In 1825 James's son, John Attwood, sold the Corngreaves Estate to the British Iron Company for the highly inflated price of £600,000, which led to the long-running court case of Small v. Attwood. In 1791 George Attwood's second son, Matthias, opened a bank in Birmingham in partnership with Isaac Spooner. He extended Hawne House and, in 1806, bought the famous Leasowes Estate, Halesowen, from Charles Hamilton for £20,000. Matthias Attwood died at Hawne in 1836, aged 90. His four sons had all left Halesowen, Thomas Attwood (1783-1856) becoming Birmingham's first MP in 1832. Matthias Attwood's daughter, Mary Anne, lived for many years at the Leasowes, but she returned to Hawne House before her death in 1872, aged 90. Hawne House was later worked as a farm by Robert Smart; later farmers there include Joseph Parkes, John Yates and William Petford

The Leasowes

The Leasowes was one of the largest farms in the hamlet of Lapal and belonged for many years to the Underhill family. In 1558, Richard Underhill leased a large property there for 1,000 years from Thomas Blount and George Tuckey. In 1660, Richard Underhill of the Leasowes was buried at Halesowen. Elijah Underhill, headmaster of Hunnington Free School until his death in 1732, was probably from the same family and was witness to a deed of 1710 when William Shenstone, formerly of Illey, but then of the Leasowes, gave land in Halesowen to his son Thomas.[5]

In 1713 Thomas Shenstone, then aged 25 and described on the licence as a butcher, married Anne, the 30-year-old daughter of William Penn of Harborough Hall, Hagley, at Pedmore. Their son William, born the following year, grew up in a prosperous household and, for a while, attended Halesowen Grammar School. His parents both died young, his father, Thomas Shenstone, in 1724, and his mother, Anne, in 1732. She and her sister Mary, who had married Thomas Dolman, rector of Broome, were co-heirs to Harborough Hall. William Shenstone, now under the guardianship of his uncle, the Rev. Dolman, was entitled to an income from his mother's estate of £300 a year, enough for him to behave like a gentleman. Shenstone was sent to Pembroke College, Oxford, in 1732, where he met several clever and genial young men, such as Richard Graves and Richard Jago, who were to remain his lifelong friends. He corresponded with them regularly in later life, describing his latest poetical contrivances and his efforts to make the Leasowes one of the finest landscape gardens in the country. Some of Shenstone's most revealing letters, however, were addressed to Henrietta, wife of Lord Luxborough, who lived at Barrels, Henley in Arden, whilst her husband remained in London. She was unduly fond of Shenstone, encouraging his literary and horticultural endeavours and indulging his social pretensions. Shenstone extended the house at the Leasowes,

93 *The Leasowes, c.1900.*

built a ruined priory in the garden and, in 1755, leased further land in Lapal from Sir George Lyttelton.[6] He induced all the gentry of the district to inspect his gardens and was even favoured by a visit from Earl Temple, of Stowe in Buckinghamshire, who was staying with the Lytteltons at Hagley Hall.

William Shenstone died at the Leasowes, lonely and impoverished, in 1763. His executor, John Hodgetts, who has been criticised for cutting down much of the timber on the estate, probably had to do so to pay Shenstone's debts. The Leasowes then had a succession of occupants who cared little for it, including Apphia Peach, the widow of the Governor of Calcutta, Joseph Peach. She left the Leasowes in 1772 after a whirlwind romance with Thomas Lyttelton, son of Lord Lyttelton, who was in need of her £20,000 fortune. In 1773, the Leasowes was purchased by Edward Horne for £8,150. He demolished Shenstone's house and built the present structure in 1778, purchasing further land at Mucklow Hill and extending the Priory Pool. In 1779, he insured the Leasowes with the Sun Fire Office for the unusually large

94 *The Leasowes, rear view, 1900.*

sum of £3,500. It comprised the dwelling house and offices, brick and slated, valued at £2,800; a stable and coach house under one roof, brick and slated, valued at £200; and a separate stable, coach house and barn, also brick and slated, valued at a further £500.[7] John Wesley, visiting the Leasowes in 1782, declared 'I never was so surprised. I have seen nothing in all England to compare with it. Such walks, such shades, such hills and dales, such lawns, such artless cascades, such waving woods as exceed all imagination'. Soon after Edward Horne sold the Leasowes in 1792 the Dudley canal was built through the estate, its huge embankment cutting the Priory Pool in two and curtailing the view of Halesowen. In 1806 Matthias Attwood, of Hawne House, bought the Leasowes for £20,000.[8] Attwood's unmarried daughter, Mary Anne Attwood, lived at the Leasowes until 1865 when the house was sold to Benjamin Gibbons for £17,000.

There is a large monument in Halesowen churchyard to Benjamin Gibbons, who was a partner in the Corbyns Hall ironworks and colliery, Kingswinford.[9] He died in 1873, in his 90th year. In 1877 his son, John Skipworth Gibbons, purchased land in Great Cornbow on which to build Halesowen Institute. He later gave the Institute to the people of Halesowen. In 1907, Halesowen Golf Club was founded, and they leased part of the Leasowes Estate for an 18-hole golf course. Edward Horne's house of 1778 later became the club house. Halesowen Urban District Council bought the estate in 1934 for £8,200, primarily to stop its development for housing. Halesowen Golf Club's lease was extended, but 38 acres of the estate were made into a public park. Halesowen Golf Club still occupies the bulk of the land, but in 1997 Dudley Metropolitan Borough was awarded a grant of £1.3 million by the Heritage Lottery Fund to restore the landscaped gardens to their former glory. Flooding in 1999 exposed the weakness of two of the dams used by Shenstone to create pools and cascades. Work was stopped and the project reassessed, but phase one of the restoration is now due for completion in 2005.

Belle Vue House

In 1783 the Birmingham ironmaster, James Male, bought a small farm at Mucklow Hill from Benjamin Wright of Birmingham, merchant.[10] He set about building a rural retreat there, insuring the uncompleted house, with two adjoining wings, for £400 in 1784.[11] James Male was evidently associated with the group of radical dissenters who got together at a Birmingham hotel in July 1791 to celebrate the fall of the Bastille two years earlier; a mob supporting 'Church and King' attacked the hotel and went on to burn down the houses of leading radicals such as Joseph Priestley. In the following days, the mob attacked gentlemen's houses further afield, and were stopped from destroying James Male's new house at Halesowen only by the timely arrival of a troop of soldiers under the command of the Earl of Aylesford.

James Male died in August 1824 aged 75. His family then let Belle Vue to Michael Grazebrook, the Stourbridge coal and ironmaster, whose daughter married

95   *Belle Vue House, c.1900.*

Ferdinando Smith of Halesowen Grange. When the Hill Tithe Award was made in 1844 the estate, comprising the house and six acres of lawns and garden, was occupied by John Meredith, a varnish manufacturer. From the 1850s to the 1880s the tenant was Edward Gem, who was followed in the 1890s by Walter Somers, the owner of the nearby Haywood Forge; Walter bought the freehold of the house in 1907 and died there in 1917.[12] In 1926, Belle Vue was bought by the Shropshire, Worcestershire & Staffordshire Electric Power Company. The original house was dwarfed by extensions in 1948, 1982 and 1990. Midlands Electricity Plc left the site in 1998, and the original Belle Vue House and some other buildings were demolished. The land was to have been developed as a business park by A.J. Mucklow & Co. Ltd, but the company has now received planning permission to build houses on the site instead.

Bundle Hill House

Bundle Hill House was a rambling 18th-century building with an overbearing pedimented façade overlooking Hales Road and the cemetery. Bundle Hill was originally the name of a furlong in High Field, one of the common arable fields of Hasbury. In 1725 Humphrey Coley of Halesowen, barber surgeon, sold half an acre of land there to Thomas Hinchley of Halesowen, brick maker. Hinchley built a house on the land, which became known as Bundle Hill House; it was bought in 1805 by John Burr of Halesowen, millwright and owner of the gun-barrel boring mill at Hayseech.[13] John Burr died in November 1805, and there is a large gravestone to his memory in Halesowen churchyard. His son John continued to live at Bundle Hill House, even during the financial troubles of 1825, when he was described as John Burr of Halesowen, ironmaster, millwright, dealer and chapman, a bankrupt. The second John Burr died in 1856, owning not only the property at Bundle Hill and the mill at Hayseech, but also the draper's shop at the bottom of High Street called Laconstone House, then occupied by Messrs Trewolla &

Connop. John Burr's son, Arthur Richard Burr, died in 1875; there is a window to his memory in Halesowen church. After this date Bundle Hill House was let to the Misses Jones, then to Henry Thompson and later to Mrs Heath. The house was sold by the Burr family in 1913 when it was described as 'that pleasantly situated freehold residence, Bundle Hill House, with garden, drive and appurtenances, and the cottage at rear with garden and appurtenances thereto belonging'.[14] Bundle Hill House was later used as a surgery by Dr C.A. Mather and Dr A.N. Fotheringham. It was demolished in about 1965.

96   *Bundle Hill House, drawn by Hans Schwarz, c.1955.*

Highfields House

Highfields House was an attractive and ornate late 18th-century house, approached by a tree-lined driveway turning west off Hales Road. Successive trade directories of Halesowen from 1900 included a note that 'Highfields Park, in the Hasbury district, is now the residence of the Rev. George Frederick Burr M.S.A. It is a commanding building of red brick, surrounded by 200 acres of land, standing on a high eminence overlooking the town, and was built in 1700 by Sir John Peshall Bart'. This myth had been started by the Rev. John Pearsall in the 1770s (see Hawne House, pp.106-7). It obviously suited later owners of Highfields House to repeat the story. In fact Highfields House was built on a piece of land in the Highfield, leased in 1767 by George Lord Lyttelton and his son Thomas Lyttelton to Elizabeth Pearsall, sister of the infamous Rev. Pearsall.[15] Elizabeth Pearsall built Highfields House soon afterwards, her builder employing the then popular 'Strawberry Hill gothic' style.

Elizabeth Pearsall's will of 1774 left her ready money, securities for money, household goods, plate, linen, china, pictures, furniture and the residue of her personal estate to her trustees, the Rev. Pynson Wilmott, vicar of Halesowen, John

97 *Highfields House, 1959.*

Cox of Cradley, iron master, George Attwood of Halesowen, ironmonger, Richard Godlin of Frankley, farmer, Ferdinando Smith of the Grange, Esquire, John Crane of Halesowen, whitener and Thomas Wright of Halesowen, gentleman, 'towards the erecting maintaining supporting and establishing of a charity school within the town of Halesowen aforesaid for the educating instructing and clothing of as many poor girls born in the said parish of Halesowen (as the income interest and produce of the residue of my said personal estate will allow and admit) in the principles of the Church of England as by law established and to read knit and work plain work'. She wanted them to appoint 'a prudent discreet woman properly qualified to be a school mistress for the said intended school and find and provide for her a convenient house for her habitation with a proper school room adjoining in the said town of Halesowen and pay unto such schoolmistress the yearly salary of ten pounds by four equal payments'. She even nominated her own servant, Jane Cutler, to be the first schoolmistress. Elizabeth Pearsall was probably as self-important as her brother, the Rev. John Pearsall, and her estate is unlikely to have been sufficient to found a girls' school. Her trustees evidently ignored her bequest, for there is no trace of an early girls' school in Halesowen.

The Pearsall family sold Highfields House in 1793 to William Powell of Halesowen, a timber merchant who had probably made his money selling wood for charcoal, which was still used in many local furnaces. William Powell also owned several houses in Great Cornbow. William Powell of Highfields died in 1825 aged 69, and was buried at Halesowen. Highfields House was inherited by William Powell's daughter, Esther Lowe Hill. She let the house to John Burr, engineer, mining agent and owner of the gun-barrel boring mill at Hayseech. He died in 1856. Later tenants included the Rev. Edward Reeve minister of Halesowen Congregational Church (1828-54), the Rev. Edwin Alfred Kempson (a relative of

Romsley's first rector, the Rev. Howard Kempson) and the Rev. James Kidd, curate of St John's, Halesowen (1864-68).

In 1871, Highfields House and 13 acres of land were sold to Alfred Burr of Halesowen, engineer, the brother of Arthur Burr of Bundle Hill House. The Burrs continued to let Highfields. Alfred Homfray, solicitor and clerk to the magistrates for Halesowen Division, lived there before he built the nearby Otterbourne Court, now used by the British Legion. His son, Jeston Homfray, married Gladys Mary, daughter of the Rev. George Frederick Burr in 1908. By 1904 Highfields was occupied by the Rev. George Frederick Burr, MSA, who died there in 1913. The Rev. Burr's widow sold Highfields house in 1919 to the Rev. Henry Charles Asgill Colvile, rector of Halesowen from 1917-36. Colvile abandoned the old Rectory in Church Street and resided at Highfields House, leading to its alternative name of the 'Old Rectory'. Highfields Park was bought by Halesowen Borough Council in 1944; the house was converted into flats, but the building was eventually demolished in about 1970.

98 *Highfields House, 1959.*

Witley Lodge

The big house on Stourbridge Road called Witley Lodge may have its origin in the 'tiled barn at Witley' referred to in a 1549 lease of the former Halesowen Abbey land to George Tuckey. In 1769 Thomas Brettell, the son of a Romsley farmer, but then a solicitor in Stourbridge, leased a house, mill and land, including Witley Barn Meadow, from George Lord Lyttelton. Brettell took advantage of Thomas Lord Lyttelton's insolvency and bought the freehold in 1775.[16] His tenants at Witley appear to have been the occupants of Shelton Mill: William Bowater, corn miller, Daniel Winwood, chapemaker, and Samuel Harris. The Witley estate also included Drew's Forge, occupied by Joseph Coley.[17] Thomas Brettell went to live at Finstall House, Stoke Prior, where he restored the old Chapel of St Godwald in 1773. He died at Finstall in 1792.

99. *Witley Lodge, Stourbridge Road, 1969*

In 1820 Thomas Brettell's granddaughter, Elizabeth, married David Homfray, the son of a Stourbridge ironmaster, and the couple set up house at Witley Lodge.[18] David Homfray was a coalmaster and may have begun the development of Witley Colliery. He died at Witley Lodge in 1870, but his successors in 1874 leased the mineral rights under the Witley estate to the Witley Colliery Company, in which various members of the Brettell and Homfray families held shares. David Homfray's youngest son, Popkin Homfray, lived at Witley Lodge until his death in 1900. The house was then occupied by Henry Jackson, manager of Witley Colliery. When the pumping engine at Old Hawne Colliery ceased working in 1921, Witley Colliery flooded and was abandoned. Witley Lodge was later tenanted by James Williams, James Wilmott, Sidney Fellows and F.P. Hands before being purchased for a road scheme in 1969, and demolished in 1973.

Chapter VII

CHURCHES AND CHAPELS

જીન્જી

Domesday Book reveals the immense power and wealth of the church in Worcestershire in 1086. Of the 1,200 hides of land listed, no fewer than 786 were held by the Church. The Bishop of Worcester, the Abbot of Evesham and the Abbot of Pershore were therefore the most important landlords in the county. Domesday Book mentions only 60 priests in 57 Worcestershire parishes, so it is remarkable to find two priests listed at Halesowen. It has been suggested that the second priest officiated at St Kenelm's, but there is no evidence for the existence of a chapel at Romsley at that early date. It is more likely that Halesowen was acting as a 'minster' church, like Kidderminster, caring for the souls of those living over a wider area than the immediate parish. The priests would be appointed by Roger of Montgomery, the new owner of the manor of Halesowen. As Earl of Shrewsbury, he took his Halesowen manor into Shropshire, but the parish remained part of the Diocese of Worcester. The Earl had no jurisdiction over Cradley, Lutley and Warley Wigorn, the hamlets which had been detached from the manor of Halesowen before Domesday. These hamlets therefore remained in Worcestershire and there is some evidence that they, like Romsley, had chapels of their own in the medieval period.

Tithes

The inhabitants of all Halesowen's hamlets, whether in Shropshire or Worcestershire, would pay a 'tithe', or tenth, of their crop to the parish church. This would pay for the maintenance of the church and provide an income for the incumbent, who would have the status of a rector: that is, a priest enjoying the full benefit of the tithes. When the manor of Halesowen was given as the endowment of Halesowen Abbey in 1215, the tithes were diverted to the upkeep of the Abbey. The abbot subsequently paid a vicar and curate to officiate in the parish church. It was also the abbot's duty, as owner of the great tithes, to maintain the chancel of the parish church, but the nave remained the responsibility of the inhabitants of the town. After the Dissolution of the Monasteries, when the assets of Halesowen Abbey came into the hands of Sir John Lyttelton, the Lyttelton family became responsible for collecting the tithes, repairing the chancel and appointing the vicar. Under the Tithe Commutation Act of 1836, tithes were to be converted into annual money payments or 'rent charges', the exact sums to be agreed between the Tithe Commissioners and the land owners. All over the country, tithe maps were drawn up to establish the liability of every plot of land; there is a tithe map for the borough of Halesowen and one for each of the hamlets. They show houses and field boundaries and are accompanied by a key listing all the owners and occupiers. Halesowen remained a vicarage until 1864, when Lord Lyttelton divided his income from tithe rent charges between the parish church and the chapels of Quinton and Romsley. Halesowen was formally termed a rectory in 1866. The building in Church Street, so long called 'The Vicarage', was now to be known as 'The Rectory'. Tithes were abolished completely under the Tithe Act of 1936.

The Medieval Church

The two priests mentioned in Domesday Book would have officiated in a large church serving a widely dispersed population. Their parish church must either have been very old or too small, for it was completely rebuilt about 1150 in the prevailing Norman style. The material used was the local red sandstone, probably brought from the old manorial quarry at Hasbury. The present west door and the arcading at the west end of the nave are clearly Norman. The ornamental arcading above the east window of the chancel and a window on the north side of the chancel (obscured by the modern vestry) are also Norman. This proves that the church was then, as it is now, about 120 feet from west to east, which is unusually long for a medieval church. The nave was about 17 feet wide, the chancel about 16 feet. The chancel arch is also Norman and built in so substantial a manner that it was probably the eastern arch of a tower which stood at the junction of the nave and chancel.

Either side of the chancel arch are fragments of the east walls of what may have been been north and south transepts, suggesting that the medieval church was cruciform in shape. These may, however, be the remains of the east walls of the north and south aisles which ran alongside the Norman arcading of the nave. A break in the masonry in the west wall shows that the south aisle was about 11 feet wide, and the base of a pier on the outside of the west wall suggests that the north aisle was of the same width. During the early 14th century, the south aisle was widened, presumably to increase the capacity of an already spacious church. The two surviving (although heavily restored) windows at the west end of this aisle are of the then popular decorated gothic style. If there was a south transept, it was absorbed into the wider aisle. The work must have involved moving the porch, with its distinctive Norman inner doorway, a little to the south, to line up with the new wall of the aisle.

In the late 14th or early 15th century, an elegant new tower was constructed, positioned halfway down the nave. It was supported on four massive piers which soar above the Norman arcading that is still preserved at the west end of the nave. Its lantern windows were built in the fashionable perpendicular gothic style. The tower was surmounted by a stone spire that tapered to a point 160 feet above the ground and was visible from many miles away. Architectural historians have speculated why the tower should have been rebuilt at this time and in this unusual position.

100   *St John's Church, Halesowen, engraved by James Green, 1746.*

The editor of the *Victoria County History* tentatively suggested that the original tower may have collapsed, taking the Norman arcading at the east end of the nave with it. His suggestion was so readily accepted that in the 1960s Nikolaus Pevsner, writing the Worcestershire volume of his *Buildings of England* series, took the theory of the collapsing tower as fact. There is no documentary evidence for the fall of the tower and the architectural evidence is that the new arcading in the nave is later than the tower. It is more likely, therefore, that the new tower was the first stage of an ambitious rebuilding plan, taken up by the inhabitants, involving the lengthening of the nave and the complete replacement of the old-fashioned Norman arcading. The chancel was not rebuilt to match, suggesting that the Abbot of Halesowen, who was responsible for maintaining the chancel, was not in favour of such an expensive project. During the late 14th century, several of the leading citizens were at loggerheads with the Abbot of Halesowen and took him to court over the level of services he demanded of them (See Chapter 1, p.11). It is quite possible, therefore, that the inhabitants built their new tower away from the chancel, where any opposition from the Abbot would be less of a hindrance.

The next step in the rebuilding plan was the replacement of the Norman arcading east of the tower with loftier pointed arches. These were surmounted by clerestory windows which gave extra light to the body of the church. The new roof of this part of the nave was leaded and could therefore be of a very shallow pitch. The line of the old, steeply-pitched tiled roof is clearly marked out on the east face of the tower, proving that the arcading and clerestory windows are of a later date than the tower. If the inhabitants had intended to replace the Norman arcading west of the tower and build more clerestory windows, they must have run out of funds, or decided that other alterations took priority.

During the 15th century, the north aisle of the church was widened. If there had been a north transept, it would have disappeared during these alterations. Here the windows are also of the later perpendicular style. The east end of this aisle may have been extended alongside the chancel later in the 15th century to provide a chantry

101   *St John's Church, Halesowen, 1975.*

chapel. Here an unusually tall perpendicular window was inserted, throwing light on the altar of St Katherine. Nearby was a stone staircase, still visible on both sides of the wall, which gave access to a rood loft running in front of St Katherine's chapel and the chancel arch, on which were hung images of Jesus on the cross and other biblical scenes. According to the surviving churchwardens' accounts of 1504-5, this rood loft was replaced at great expense.

The last addition to the church before the Reformation was a new aisle, the building of which commenced in 1531. This must have been an extension on the east end of the existing south aisle. Eighteenth-century drawings of St John's Church show two square-headed perpendicular windows in the part of the south aisle which ran alongside the chancel. One of these windows (heavily restored) survives today. The building of this extension is referred to in the Churchwardens' Accounts of 1531, when a bargain was struck with Edward Nichols and his fellow 'for the making of the aisle of the church'. In the next three years there are large payments for carrying timber, stone, sand, lime, lead and nails for the building work. These expenses were met by donations and by successive 'church ales', which were fund-raising events where the church made a handsome profit by brewing ale specially for consumption on the day. In 1534, there is a note of a final payment of £7 to the carpenters. There is a record in 1549 of the payment to the churchwardens of 3s. 4d. from the executors of John Parkes of Cakemore 'for his burial in the new aisle'.[1] At the east end of this new extension was the altar of St Stephen. Wealthier inhabitants left money in their wills for candles for the altars of St Mary, St Katherine and St Stephen. The Churchwardens Accounts list regular and substantial payments for beeswax, and costs incurred by the priest in writing up his prayers to be said for the salvation of such donors.

The Reformation

Had the churchwardens delayed construction of the new aisle for a few more years, they would have had access to an almost inexhaustible source of cheap building materials. After the seizure of Halesowen Abbey by Henry VIII's agents in 1539, and its sale to Sir John Dudley, the new tenant, George Tookey, was free to strip any surplus buildings of valuable lead and timber and use the remainder as a stone quarry. Some of the fittings were saved; the rood screen, the organ and an image of Saint Kenelm were brought from the Abbey church and installed at St John's. Henry VIII's break from Rome might have been prompted by political necessity, but Edward VI's Protestant ministers took the English Reformation forward with genuine religious zeal. In 1549, they demanded that all altars in English churches be replaced by communion tables, all idolatrous images removed and a new English prayer book used in services. The change is fully documented in Halesowen with payments of 14d. 'for pulling down the high altar and Saint Mary's altar and bearing out the stones' and 16d. 'for making the communion board and other necessaries'. There are repeated payments for white-liming the church, suggesting that all the images and wall paintings were covered over, and several large payments to a glazier,

who presumably replaced any offending stained glass. There is even a payment in
1551 of 3s. 4d. for a new service book.

On the accession of Catholic Queen Mary in 1553, the churchwardens faced
further expense, to reinstate the altars they had so recently destroyed. The wife
of the new occupant of the Abbey proved her loyalty to the new regime by the
contribution of 12d. 'of Mistress Tokey toward the making of the altar'. In 1558,
the first year of the reign of Protestant Queen Elizabeth, however, the whole
process was reversed, with payments for taking down the altar and making another
communion table. Soon there are entries in the churchwardens' accounts for buying
'the communion book at Dudley' and 'for taking down the rood loft' (the image
of Christ above the chancel screen).[2]

Although England then settled down to 40 years of rule by a determinedly
Protestant Queen, the manor of Halesowen was purchased in 1558 by John Lyttelton
of Frankley, an avowed Catholic. With the manor went the right to appoint the
vicars of Halesowen. Although Catholic landlords could not appoint openly Catholic
priests to their parishes, they might have leaned towards the high church rather
than the Puritan wing of the Church of England. In 1601 the Lyttelton estates
were confiscated by the Crown, John Lyttelton having been implicated in Essex's
rebellion. His brother Humphrey Lyttelton was later executed for his part in the
Gunpowder Plot in 1605. The family learnt its lesson: in pleading for the return of
the family estates, John Lyttelton's widow, Meriel, undertook to bring up her son
Thomas as a Protestant.

102   *West doorway, St
John's Church, Halesowen,
1961.*

The Civil War

The Church of England took a new direction in 1633, when Charles I appointed William Laud as Archbishop of Canterbury. The Halesowen churchwardens no doubt implemented Laud's decree that communion tables or altars should be positioned in the chancel and that the area be railed off. The 'communion rails' as they became known were ostensibly to stop dogs straying into this hallowed space, but to the Puritans, who wanted to take communion kneeling around the communion table, this was an affront and smacked of popery. Laud became one of the most disliked of Charles's ministers and his attempt to introduce the English Prayer Book in Scotland precipitated a war with the Scots. It was Charles's struggle with Parliament over how to raise money for the Scottish campaign, and, more to the point, who should have control of the troops, which finally precipitated the English Civil War. The lord of the manor, Sir Thomas Lyttelton, was an active supporter of the King, but many tradesmen in the town had close links with Birmingham, which was a Parliamentary stronghold. The Royalists upheld the right of the bishops to rule the Church of England; many Parliamentarians favoured a Presbyterian or democratic church, similar to the Scottish model. The national struggle was played out in Halesowen with the vicar, Thomas Littelton, having to leave the parish in 1647 and make way for a Puritan minister, Edward Paston. In 1648 Paston's name appeared in support of 'a testimony of the Ministers in the Province of Salop to the truth of Jesus Christ and to the Solemn League and Covenant, as also against the Errors, Heresies and Blasphemies of these times, and the toleration of them'. With the restoration of Charles II in 1660, Edward Paston was in turn forced to leave the vicarage, and was replaced by John Westwood, a nephew of the former vicar, Thomas Littelton. Paston remained resident in Halesowen, untroubled by Charles II's Act of Parliament forbidding ejected ministers from preaching within five miles of their former parish.[3] In his will of 1695, Edward Paston left 'my study of books to such of my grandsons John Paston and Samuel Paston or to which of them shall be brought up a scholar for the ministry'.

Changes in St John's Church during the 18th century were prompted more by the need to accommodate the growing population of the town than by changes in doctrine or liturgy. The wealthier inhabitants of Halesowen paid the churchwardens rents for private pews, which were then handed down in their families. Poorer families were catered for in 1772 with the construction of a gallery, that stretched across the church from north to south, passing under the arches of the tower. Congregations at this time expected a good long sermon, so there was a 'three-decker' pulpit in front of the chancel arch. This comprised a clerk's desk on the lower level, a lectern on the second level, from which the vicar conducted the service, and the pulpit at the top, from which he delivered his sermon. Over the pulpit was a sounding board, which helped project the vicar's words to the congregation.

By 1820, the churchwardens must have been discussing further alterations to the church, because the prolific church architect, Francis Goodwin, prepared elegant plans and a printed specification to show how the church could be enlarged. He

Vicars of Halesowen		*Rectors*	
1282	Richard Tinctor of Hales	1836	Richard Brindley Hone, MA, Archdeacon of Worcester
1282	Robert of Crowle	1881	Hon Francis Godolphin Pelham, MA, later Earl of Chichester
1286	William Russell of Doddel	1884	Charles Codrington Nation, MA
1306	William of Frankley	1893	John Charles Hill, MA, Canon of Worcester, later Bishop of Hulme
1311	Philip of Bromwich		
1349	Richard of Hampton		
1369	Roger of Ree		
1375	John Pool	1909	Ronald Symes, MA
1395	Henry Frebody	1912	Christopher William Wordsworth, MA
1425	William Edgbaston		
1468	Richard Hull	1917	Henry Charles Asgill Colvile, MA, Canon of Worcester, Rural Dean
1487	John Saunders		
1501	Roger Walsall	1936	John Timothy Davies, MA, Canon of Worcester, Proctor in Convocation, Rural Dean
1542	John Legh, A.M.		
1559	William Allen		
1581	Humphrey Lyttleton, BA	1952	Patrick Blakiston, MA
1584	Ralph Mallet	1959	John Charles Williams, BA, Canon of Worcester, Archdeacon of Dudley, later Archdeacon of Worcester
1598	Edward Danner		
1620	Thomas Lyttleton, MA		
1653	Edward Paston		
1662	John Westwood, BA		
1676	Francis Pierce, MA	1970	William Kenneth Blackburn, MA Canon of Worcester
1685	William Hume		
1696	Thomas Jukes	1978	Christopher Lionel Varley Atkinson, AKC. Canon of Worcester, Rural Dean of Dudley, first Team Ministry Rector, 1980
1719	John Amphlett, MA		
1731	Josiah Durant		
1732	Pynson Wilmot, BA		
1784	Samuel Griffith, DD		
1788	William Sutton, LIT	1989	John Keith Kimber, BSc.
1805	George Biggs, MA	1993	John Everest

proposed to demolish the whole of the fabric east of the tower and to create a spacious 'preaching box' nave, with a small chancel beyond in the form of an apse. The west end was to be used as a grand entrance to the church. The churchwardens did not proceed with the scheme, but in 1825 Goodwin produced further plans, showing how seating capacity could be raised by the installation of more galleries in the existing building. Francis Goodwin's second plan was also rejected.[4]

In 1836, the Rev. Richard Brindley Hone began his 45 years' service as vicar, and later rector, of Halesowen. He was the sort of man who got things done, and in 1838 he employed the Birmingham architect Richard Hussey to increase accommodation by installing galleries over the north and south aisles. This required the raising of

103 Interior of St John's Church, Halesowen, 1960.

the outer walls and the construction of flat rooves over the aisles. At the same time, the Norman chancel arch was raised several feet, although most of the detailed stonework was re-used.[5] Richard Hussey was later to work on the 1846 restoration of St Kenelm's Church, Romsley. St John's Church was reopened after these changes on 8 September 1839; the alterations are said to have cost £3,000 and to have increased the capacity of the church to 1,700 seats. On 30 March 1851, when the Religious Census was taken, however, there were only 311 adults and 323 Sunday scholars at the morning service; 319 and 176 respectively came to the afternoon service, and 260 attended the evening service. The Rev. Hone claimed that the numbers were, for various reasons, much below average, but he was not one of the many Anglican priests who blamed the poor turnout on the weather.[6]

During the Rev. Richard Brindley Hone's incumbency, the Church of England went through a period of radical change which was to express itself in church liturgy and in the design and restoration of churches. The reformers' object was to take the church back to the perceived purity of worship prior to the Reformation. Church architecture should therefore be modelled on the gothic styles in vogue before the 1530s. In 1871, the Rev. Hone engaged the London architect Henry Curzon to suggest options for the rearrangement of the interior of St John's Church. The result was the removal of the west gallery and the further raising of the chancel arch, although the bulk of the stonework was retained. In 1873, he obtained a faculty from the Bishop of Worcester to remove the galleries of 1838 and to make other alterations to provide free seating elsewhere in the church. He employed the most famous church architect, Sir George Gilbert Scott (1811-78), to supervise the work. The galleries were removed and new oak seating and chairs were provided to accommodate 800 people. The old three-decker pulpit was replaced with the present structure. The work cost over £6,000. The Rev. Hone, as rector, paid for alterations to the chancel. The huge monument to John Halliday of the Leasowes was removed to the back of the church, leaving more space for holding the communion. A new four-light east window was built in the Early-English style in memory of the Rev. Hone's late wife. The church was reopened following these alterations on 26 May 1875.

The Rev. George Brindley Hone died on 5 May 1881 aged 76. He did not live to see the completion of the final stage of restoration: the reduction of the outer walls of the aisles to their original height, the replacement of the flat rooves over the aisles with new pitched rooves and the building of an additional south aisle. This work was organised by George Gilbert Scott's son, John Oldrid Scott, at further cost of £4,500. The debts incurred by the churchwardens during the rebuilding programme were met by successive appeals, and a grand bazaar held in Birmingham Town Hall in October 1882. The newly extended church, officially opened on 9 April 1883, could now accommodate 1,100 people.[7]

During the 19th century, the church responded to the growth of nonconformity not only by extending the parish church, but also by building new churches in areas of growing population. Christ Church, Quinton, was built in 1840 to serve the hamlet of Ridgacre. It had seating for 600 worshippers. On the morning of 30 March 1851, there were 95 in the general congregation and 51 attending the Sunday School. In the afternoon there were 200 in the general congregation and 38 at the Sunday School. Some in the Church of England thought the lack of working-class people in the congregation was because they were afraid to come to church in their ordinary clothes. Mission churches were therefore established at Short Cross and at Birmingham Street. St Margaret's Church, Hasbury, was built in 1908 with 500 seats. A temporary church was built at Lapal in 1950 and the present St Peter's Church, Lapal, was opened in 1964.

Nonconformists

It is unusual for an industrial town not to have an early tradition of dissent from the Church of England. Perhaps when separate congregations were being formed in other towns, the preaching of Edward Paston, the ejected Commonwealth

104 *Church Street and the Rectory, 1957. The Rectory was largely rebuilt by the Rev. Richard Brindley Hone, and enlarged by his successor, The Rev. Francis Godolphin Pelham. It was demolished in 1961.*

minister, was sufficient to satisfy any independent spirits in the town. The Halesowen churchwardens made a return to the Bishop of Worcester in 1676 claiming that, out of the 554 inhabitants of the parish over the age of 16, only three were papists and four were dissenters of other kinds. Perhaps some Halesowen nonconformists travelled to Oldbury, where the old chapel, established by the Church before the Reformation, had been taken over by a Presbyterian congregation during the Commonwealth. In 1705, the vicar of Halesowen had to admit that the chapel there was still served by nonconforming ministers. Some Halesowen dissenters may have joined the Presbyterians in Cradley, who built a meeting house at Cradley Forge in 1707. John Pearsall of Halesowen, yeoman, was one of the original trustees. This group flourished and built the much larger Park Lane Chapel in 1796.

105   *The Mission Church, Birmingham Street, awaiting demolition, 1966.*

Halesowen Congregational Church

In 1804 a group of tradesmen began to hold independent meetings in a barn behind the house of Benjamin Hodgkins, in Birmingham Street. Early trustees of this congregation included Joseph Harris, maltster (and partner in the nearby button factory), Joseph Granger the elder, breeches maker, Joseph Granger the younger, mercer, Benjamin Brettell, tailor, Benjamin Hodgkins, hoop maker, Joseph Brettell, shoemaker and David Darby, farmer. In 1811, they built a fine new chapel at the corner of Hagley Street and Cornbow. The land was purchased from Walter Woodcock and the building costs were £800.[8] By 1828 the congregation had outgrown the accommodation and a gallery was installed above the doorway. Side galleries were added a few years later. The Congregational minister, Edward Reeve, then living at Highfields House, reported that on 30 March 1851 there were 158 adults and 219 Sunday scholars at the morning service, 184 and 200 respectively came to the afternoon service, and 262 attended the evening service. These results show that the Congregational Church was by far the most successful of Halesowen's nonconformist churches. From time to time, new trustees were appointed. A trust deed of 1886 gives a further impression of the people who supported the church, with new trustees including Thomas Harris the button manufacturer, now living at Boldmere in Sutton Coldfield, George Allan, of Corngreaves Hall, ironmaster, Henry Parish, nailmaster, George Augustus Weston, solicitor's clerk, David Blow Harris of Boldmere, fancy leather manufacturer, John Benjamin Parkes, tailor, Osmond Young, tailor, John Jones, carpenter and Francis Hodgkins, wooden hoop and hurdle manufacturer.

In 1909, A new Sunday school was built on land in Hagley Road, purchased from Frederick Tench Goodman. The architect was A.T. Butler, who also designed the Cosy Corner Cinema and the hairdresser's shop in the Bull Ring. The site in Hagley Road was to prove useful, for in 1960 the old chapel in Great Cornbow was sold for redevelopment and a new church was built in front of the Sunday School.

Methodism

John Wesley visited Halesowen as early as 1770, when he addressed a large crowd in Cradley. The stone on which he stood to preach at Dungeon Head is preserved at High Town Ragged School. A group of Methodists had been formed in 1766 and built their own meeting house in 1768. The group diminished and was forced to sell their chapel in 1786, but, experiencing a revival in 1796, they bought the meeting house at Cradley Forge, formerly used by the Presbyterians. Methodism also gained an early foothold at Quinton, where a congregation was formed by a gentleman farmer called Ambrose Foley, who had first heard Wesley preach in London; John Wesley visited Foley at Quinton Farm in 1781. The chair he stood on to address

106 *Congregational Church, Great Cornbow, built 1811.*

the large crowd was preserved locally as a Methodist icon. John Wesley presented Mrs Foley with a blue and white tea set, the teapot decorated with portraits of John Wesley and 15 of the preachers who travelled with him on the Staffordshire Circuit. Ambrose Foley subsequently built a Wesleyan chapel near to the turnpike house at Quinton and John Wesley himself preached at the opening in 1786. This chapel survived until 1878, when it was replaced by a much larger building on the same site. This continued in use until 1935 when the congregation joined with the neighbouring Primitive Methodist Church. Quinton Farm was demolished in the 1930s to make way for the *Kings Highway* public house.

During its two and a half centuries of existence, Methodism has divided over policy, but never over doctrine. These divisions were healed in 1932 with the three branches of Methodism represented in Halesowen; Wesleyans, Primitive Methodists and New Connexion Methodists joined together in the present-day Methodist Church. Methodism was organised on the circuit system, where a group of churches in the same area was led by a travelling preacher, an ordained minister sent by the national Conference, who stayed for a year or two and then moved on. Local preachers conducted services and baptisms.

New Connexion Methodists

No Methodist meeting house seems to have been established in the borough of Halesowen until a small chapel was built on the corner of Brook Street and Birmingham Street in 1825.[9] This may have been a Wesleyan Chapel, but, after a bitter dispute in 1835 over the training of preachers, many Wesleyan congregations, including that at Cradley Forge and possibly the Halesowen chapel as well, joined the Methodist New Connexion. The minister in 1837 was the Rev. Peter Trewin. Under the ministry of the Rev. W Seaton in 1841, the Methodist New Connexion congregation in Birmingham Street bought a plot of land on Stourbridge Road from Lord Lyttelton. On Monday 13 June 1842, after parading through the town, a 'great concourse' of people met on the site for the stone laying. 'The multitude listened with most marked attention; and though most of them were very poor, the collection at the close amounted to more than nine pounds in addition to fifty-two pounds previously subscribed, and expended in the purchase of the land.' Their handsome new church, called Zion Chapel, opened in December 1842. The trustees at this time were William Pardoe, nail warehouseman, George Harris, carpenter, William Corbett, shingler, Henry White from Islington, nail maker, Henry Chatwin, shopkeeper, Heber Franklin, nailer, Thomas Yeomans, labourer and Richard Hackett, nailer. The church was on the Stourbridge Circuit.

On 30 March 1851, there were 40 adults and 53 Sunday scholars at the morning service; 56 and 57 respectively came to the afternoon service, and 76 attended the evening service. The chapel steward, William Pardoe of Birmingham Street, nail warehouseman, claimed that this was below the average attendance. The building remained a Methodist church until its closure in 1979. After its purchase and renovation by Emery Estates Ltd, the building was leased by the Zion Pentecostal Church, which later moved to the former Webb Ivory factory in Little Cornbow. The old Zion chapel is now divided into offices called Church Court, and is a listed building.

Primitive Methodists

The Primitive Methodist Church grew out of the Wesleyan Church, but its special style of direct preaching at large outdoor meetings attracted many local nailers to their cause. The Primitive Methodists built their first chapel at Hasbury in 1837, which was followed by chapels at Quinton (1840), Halesowen (1848), Short Cross (1868), Hayseech (1870), and the Shenstone (1894).

The Primitive Methodist Church at Hasbury started in the early 1830s with meetings in Cherry Tree Lane at the home of Josiah Male. The first chapel was built in 1837 on the edge of a field called Red Leasowes. On 30 March 1851 there appears to have been no morning service, but in the afternoon, 90 adults and 75 children attended, and 83 adults and 20 children came in the evening. John Ball, the manager, stated that the average number attending in the previous 12 months was 150 adults and 70 children in the afternoon and 130 adults and 38 children in the evening. A new chapel was built in 1865. The organ was played in the 1880s by Charles Parish, who ran a music shop in Hagley Road, Halesowen. He later moved to be organist at Blackheath, and was killed one day on returning home down Mucklow Hill. In 1946 land adjoining the 1861 building was purchased. It was here that a new church was erected in 1970 at a cost of £20,000, which was partly met by the proceeds from the sale of Shenstone Methodist Church, which closed in 1959. Hasbury Methodist Church was considerably extended in 1985; part of

107 *Methodist New Connexion Church, Stourbridge Road, 1976.*

the £55,000 cost was raised by the sale of Zion chapel, which had closed in 1979. In the late 1990s, however, problems with the 1970 building began to show, so it was decided to build the present Hasbury Methodist Church, which was opened in 2000 having cost £400,000. This sum was raised in a similar fashion; partially by the sale of Hayseech Methodist Church, which closed in 1991. The church is strong and continues to flourish.

The first Primitive Methodist chapel in the centre of Halesowen was built at the bottom of Birmingham Street in 1848. On 30 March 1851, there were 110 adults and 81 Sunday scholars at the morning service, 140 and 77 respectively came to the afternoon service, and 150 attended the evening service. The chapel steward, John Baker, a gas fitter living at

108 *Hasbury Methodist Church, 1966.*

Rumbow, did not fill in the average numbers attending during the previous months. In 1868 the minister, the Rev. William Wright, wrote in the *Primitive Methodist Magazine* that 'the Society in this place is doing well in good things. A splendid chapel is in the course of erection. The trustees have worked well in raising £100 for the site of land and £50 more at the stone laying. The chapel will be the finest and neatest building in the town. Our prospects here are bright and cheery.' A notable member of Birmingham Street Primitive Methodist Church was the Rev. William Jones, who was born at Hawne Bank in 1834. He worked in a nail shop as a young man and entered the ministry in 1855, serving first at Ludlow, and later in 19 other circuits, including Stepney Green, Manchester, Birmingham, Derby, and Sunderland, before returning to Halesowen in 1901. He was known as 'The Enchanting Gospel Orator' and the power of his preaching was such that he could hold the attention of huge congregations for several hours. He was appointed President of the Primitive Methodist Conference at the time of Queen Victoria's Diamond Jubilee and he attended a banquet at Buckingham Palace. Another well known preacher who started in Birmingham Street Primitive Methodist Church was the Rev. Walter Tildesley, who emigrated to America in 1923 and had an outstanding ministry there. For the last ten years of his ministry he served a large Methodist church near the White House, in Washington DC. He last came to Halesowen in 1967 when he shared the pulpit at Hasbury Methodist Church with his lifelong friend, and fellow local preacher, Ben Bissell. Other significant members of this church were Benjamin Marsland, the manager of the Halesowen and Hasbury Industrial Co-operative Society, and

Walter Seeley, china and glass dealer, Hagley Street.[10] Birmingham Street Methodist Church survived until the 1980s, when the congregation joined with the United Reformed Church at Hagley Road to form the Halesowen United Church. The Birmingham Street building is now a restaurant called Benjamin's, named after Sir Benjamin Hingley, of Hatherton Lodge, Drews Holloway, who was the one time MP for the town and son of Noah Hingley, the Netherton ironmaster; he also laid the foundation stone of the chapel,

Shenstone Primitive Methodist Church was built at the instigation of John Jones, of Prospect Place, a well known local preacher, and member of the Birmingham Street Church. When a divergence of opinion arose, and he failed to get his own way, he encouraged a large number to leave Birmingham Street and found a new society. Early meetings were held in his house, but the Shenstone chapel was constructed in 1894 using £200 of his own money. He was an autocrat, but he twice received the thanks of conference 'for his munificent gifts'. In 1907 he was President of the Halesowen and District Free Church Council. Caleb Guest, who owned a music shop on the corner of Summer Hill and Laurel Lane, was a member of this church. He traded in pipe organs, and gave a pipe organ to the chapel; when he fell out with the church sometime later, however, he took the pipe organ with him. One lady who was so incensed at what he was doing that she stuck her scissors in the bellows, and the church gates were locked to prevent him from getting it out easily. The church closed in 1959, and before its demolition due to road widening and the creation of the Shenstone island it was used as a tyre warehouse.

When all these Primitive Methodist Churches were being formed, they were members of the Dudley Circuit, with 17 other churches, ranging from Oldbury to Brierley Hill. 'Hailey Green' appears on a Dudley Circuit plan (the name still used today for a three-monthly programme of preachers and their preaching appointments) for November to January 1832-3. As the number of churches multiplied, the Brierley Hill Circuit was formed from the Dudley Circuit, the Old Hill Circuit from the Brierley Hill, and the Hasbury and Halesowen Circuit from the Old Hill one in 1878. The churches at that time were Hasbury, Birmingham Street, Short Cross, Lower Hagley, Islington, Shelton, and Illey.

109 *Primitive Methodist Church, Birmingham Street, 1974.*

In 1888 a special circuit committee was called when three members of Hasbury Primitive Methodist Church – Joseph Willetts and John Brown, local preachers, and Benjamin Bissell, senior Sunday School superintendent and chapel keeper – held an open-air meeting at Spring Hill, at the same time as the ordinary evening service was being held in the Hasbury chapel. This matter caused such agitation that the minister was forced to move his residence from Hasbury to Halesowen, and Hasbury, Shenstone, and Romsley left the Circuit to join the Cradley Heath Primitive Methodist Circuit. Birmingham Street followed them in 1888. The remaining societies – Woodgate, Hayseech, Short Cross and Illey societies – were formed into the Halesowen Circuit. In 1899 Hasbury, Hagley, Shenstone and Romsley rejoined the Circuit which became 'Hasbury and Halesowen Circuit'. Birmingham Street rejoined in 1909. Zion, which had stayed with the Stourbridge churches after the Methodist union, eventually joined the Circuit in 1965. The name was changed to the 'Halesowen Circuit' and now comprises Hasbury, Romsley and Short Cross.

Short Cross Primitive Methodist Church had its beginnings in 1867 when four members started meeting in a house in the Gibbet Lane area (Alexandra Road), and then sought permission to build a schoolroom. On 12 March 1867, a piece of land was purchased for £44 4s. 0d. and the first building was erected. The first trustees were George Blease, William Walker, Sidney Smith, Josiah Yates, Samuel Smart, John Adams, William Etheridge, and Edward Crompton. The *Primitive Methodist Magazine* of 1868 has a report from Short Cross: 'Here we have purchased the land, and a good schoolroom is in the course of erection. There is a rising population in the neighbourhood and our prospects for a good society are very cheery.' Not much is known of these early beginnings but George Blease was a very devoted member and benefactor. William Walker, a brickmaker whose brickworks were in Belle Vale, supplied the bricks. William Southwell, a local preacher and Sunday school teacher, looked after the new chapel. A new church was built in 1891. The pipe organ, purchased from Nicholson & Lord, Organ Builders of Walsall, for £235 and installed in 1900, is still in use today, although it is a little extended from its original form. Their original estimate survives and is addressed to Mr John Dancer, The Highlands, Halesowen, a boot and shoe manufacturer. Numbers continued to grow and in 1908 the church was extended at the rear to meet the 1868 building. In 1935, a new church was built at a cost of £2,000, designed by Stanley Beach, architect of Halesowen and built by local builders Messrs J.M. Tate and Son, of Cradley. The former church was used as the schoolroom until a new schoolroom was built in 1979 at a cost of £15,000. The church continues to grow and further premises were built in 1995, called 'The 1868 Room', because they were built on part of the foundations of the original 1868 building.

The Baptist Church

The house of William Sadler of Halesowen was licensed as a Baptist meeting house in 1744, but this congregation does not appear to have lasted many years. A Baptist church was, however, built at Cradley in 1788. The Baptist Church at

110 *Baptist Church, Stourbridge Road, 1976.*

Carter's Lane, Lapal, was built in 1811 on land leased by a local Baptist named Joseph Perry. Financial support was given by the Baptist Church at Bond Street, Birmingham. Despite its rural situation, on 30 March 1851, there were 40 adults and 41 Sunday scholars at the morning service, and 41 and 42 respectively came to the afternoon service. The original building on Carter's Lane survived until 1939, when a larger church was built to serve the growing population of this part of Halesowen. Baptists in Halesowen had probably been meeting at Caleb Bloomer's Ragged School since 1867 (see Chapter 8, p.138). The merger of the Ragged School with the British School in 1878 was probably the reason why they built their own church on Stourbridge Road in that year. A much larger church was built in front of the first building in 1899. The Baptists sold their church in the 1980s to Eric Emery, who converted it into offices; the congregation now meets in what was their Sunday School, next door.

Chapter VIII

SCHOOLS AND SCHOOLMASTERS

❧ ❦

With a wealthy abbey and a large parish church serving a very wide area there would have been plenty of clergymen in Halesowen who could supplement their income by teaching the sons of farmers and tradesmen how to write good English and keep accurate accounts. If Halesowen Abbey had ever been such a centre of learning in the community, its good influence did not survive Henry VIII's Dissolution of the Monasteries. Several parishioners came to see the need for education in the town and left small bequests towards the founding of a school. John Russell gave £50 for the poor and a free school, which he was owed on security of a bond dated 14 September 1632. John Pearsall the elder of Hawne, yeoman, in his will of 1644, gave 'towards the erecting and maintaining of a school in Halesowen aforesaid and for paying for the schooling of poor children there the sum of five pounds of lawful English money to be so employed at the discretion of my heirs, the Vicar of Halesowen for the time being, and High Bailiff of the Borough there'. Until such time as a school was commenced, he instructed that the money should be used 'for the best advantage and that the interest or benefit thereof shall be yearly distributed on Good Friday to such poor people of the town of Halesowen and the hamlets of Hawne and Hasbury as shall be in most distress'. None of these bequests, however, provided sufficient funds to found a school.

111 *The old Grammar School in the 18th century.*

Inquisition as to Charities 1652

Under an Act of Parliament of 1601, intended to redress the inappropriate employment of lands, goods and stocks of money hitherto given to certain charitable uses, the Lord Chancellor was able to appoint commissioners to make enquiries into local charitable donations. Such an inquisition was held in Halesowen in 1652 and directed that 'certain rents of land in Halesowen and elsewhere, found to have been given for some charitable use, but what particular use was not known', be applied to the maintenance of a free school and a master for the children of inhabitants to be taught to read English grammar and literature. Accordingly, 17 of the leading citizens were brought together as the Feoffees of the School of Halesowen, to appoint the schoolmaster and collect the rents from the properties allocated for the maintenance of the school. Its members were Thomas Haden, Thomas Shaw, John Lea, Raphael Taylor, Richard Hadley, Richard Guest, John Wight, John Hadley, William Parkes, George Low, William Wight, William Grove, Oliver Shaw, Richard Lowbridge, Henry Grove, John Mucklow, Richard Haden, Richard Ford and Richard Underhill. The first schoolmaster, appointed sometime between 1652 and 1660, was John Wright.[1]

Amongst the property listed in 1652 as having already been given for charitable purposes was a cottage with three acres of land lying in the common field called the New Field, and a piece of enclosed land called St Mary's Close. This was the house and land subsequently occupied rent free by successive masters of the Free School. They taught in a new schoolroom, built to the west of the cottage. It had a three-light gothic window facing on to the road which became known as Grammar School Lane. Another valuable property listed at the 1652 enquiry was 'a bark mill house and barn in Halesowen and an acre of land in Witley Field in the said parish'. This had probably been given to the town by William Wight, tanner, who as early as 1614 had charged his property in Cornbow, called the 'Bankhouse', with the annual payment of £1 per year to the poor.

The Wight family were by far the greatest benefactors of the Free School. In his will of 23 September 1660, William Wight of Cornbow, yeoman, gave to the Feoffees of the School

> All those two messuages cottages or tenements together with all shops gardens and backsides to them or either of them belonging or appertaining with their and every of their appurtenances situate and being in Prickingham Street in Halesowen and now or late were in the several possessions or occupations of John Wright, William Rowe and John Underhill or their assigns unto the use and behoof of the said Feoffees for and towards the maintenance of a schoolmaster for his teaching educating and bringing up in learning poor children within the said Borough of Halesowen.

These two houses produced a considerable income and were situated at the top of Peckingham Street, near to its corner with Birmingham Street.

Even with the Free School legally established and adequately endowed, it was not easy to secure the services of a reliable schoolmaster. In 1663, Edward Paston, John Pearsall, Henry Grove and the other Feoffees appointed Owen Williams to the mastership. In 1665 the Vicar and Churchwardens appealed to the Bishop of Worcester to revoke Williams' licence to teach, having received 'many sad complaints made unto us by our parishioners (to our great loss and discredit) of the neglect of our Free School'. They accused Williams of 'idly and carelessly neglecting, and stubbornly refusing to discharge his duty in the said school to the children of our parish after several friendly and brotherly admonitions from the Minister and Feoffees'.[2]

Many of the subsequent masters of the Free School were also curates of local churches, like the Rev. Benjamin Lea, curate of Rowley Regis, who was appointed headmaster in 1733. His son, William Arch Lea (1732-1802), was curate of St Kenelm's. The Rev. Robert Robertson, curate of Harborne, was appointed headmaster in 1796, and also became a curate at St John's, Halesowen. In 1811, Robertson was criticised by the Feoffees for neglecting the school. At an inquiry conducted by the Charity Commissioners in 1823, it was found that Robertson had had no classical scholars for 15 years, and that many of his 57 pupils, being sons of farmers, were absent during seedtime and harvest. Tuition was free, but books and paper were bought by the parents who also paid a shilling in each of the winter terms for heating the school. The school house was described as a commodious habitation with a good garden and six acres of land which the master occupied rent free. The income from the various endowments was £105 per year, from which the master paid for the repair of the premises and the £30 salary of an usher or assistant. The Rev. Robertson died in December 1824.

112 *Grammar School Lane, 1966, showing the school buildings erected in 1864 and the Drill Hall, all of which were demolished for the building of a traffic island in 1973.*

During the long tenure of the next master, John Lomax, school numbers declined even further and, after his death in 1863, the school closed for several months. With the appointment of a new schoolmaster, the Rev. C.J. Wood, the Rev. Richard Brindley Hone, Chairman of the Feoffees, pushed through a new scheme of management for the school in 1864.[3] The old schoolmaster's house was demolished and a new wing, fronting Grammar School Lane, was added on the north side of the old schoolroom. In order to fund the new building, some of the school's endowments were sold, thereby reducing the income. This was made up by charging 10s. per quarter for boys up to 12 years of age, and 15s. for older boys. The sons of the labouring classes paid a reduced fee of 5s. per quarter. The new fees proved very unpopular and, by 1883, only 14 pupils remained. The next master, Thomas Disney, increased the fees and took pupils from the neighbouring towns, increasing numbers to 70 by 1888 but, by the end of his headship in 1904, numbers had again declined to 23 pupils.

Under the Education Act of 1902, County Councils were able to contribute to the maintenance of existing grammar schools. The injection of cash and support from Worcestershire County Council enabled the school to admit girls and to put up fine new buildings in 1908. In 1928, Halesowen Grammar School ceased to be 'aided' by the County Council, which afterwards 'maintained' the school. This led

113   *Halesowen Grammar School: new buildings erected in 1908.*

114   *Halesowen Grammar School extension, built in 1931.*

to the building of the elegant new extension of 1931, designed by A.T. Butler, a former pupil. The school now had the capacity to educate 450 children.

Under the 1944 Education Act the school leaving age was raised to 15 and all fees were abolished. Pupils would be admitted to grammar schools and technical schools only on passing an entrance examination. Although 20 per cent of Halesowen children passed the 'eleven plus', critics suggested that labelling the remaining 80 per cent as failures was counter-productive. The 1964 Labour Government required education authorities to prepare plans for comprehensive secondary education. As a first step towards a comprehensive school in the town, Halesowen Grammar School and Halesowen Technical School amalgamated in 1966.

Headmasters of the Grammar School

	Date of appointment
John Wright	?
Thomas Haughten	5 September 1659
Owen Williams	27 June 1663
Josiah Reade	2 October 1665
Rev. Robert Durant	1693
Rev. Joseph Chillingworth	5 May 1707
Rev. Joseph Thorp, BA	1 September 1707
Rev. John Jacob, BA	4 October 1721
Rev. Thomas Stinton, BA	8 January 1723
Joseph Hipkis	28 April 1725
Rev. Benjamin Lea	27 March1733
Rev. Matthew Wilmot	11 July 1763
Rev. Henry Sanders	17 July 1771
Rev. John Parkes, BA	15 June 1785
Rev. Robert Robertson.	18 April 1796
John Lomax	22 December 1824
Rev. J.C. Wood	7 November 1863
Rev. J.H. Richardson	21 December 1866
W. F. Matthews, MA	13 December 1871
Thomas Disney, MA	17 December 1883
Ralph Dickinson, BA	29 March 1904
Wilfred A. Grace, MA	1 September 1929
E. Harold Mander, MA	1 September 1939
Clifford Emmott, BA, B.Litt.	13 April 1950

The National Schools

During the 19th century both the Church of England and the nonconformist churches developed their Sunday schools and attempted to provide part or full-time education for the children of their respective congregations. The National School erected in

115   *Church of England School, Church Street, 1966.*

Church Street in 1838 was supported by the National Society for the Education of the Poor in the Principles of the Established Church. A National School was built in Cradley in 1854, and similar foundations were made at Hasbury in 1870 and at Long Lane, Hill and Cakemore in 1873.

British Schools

British Schools were founded in most industrial towns to provide education for the children of nonconformist families, free from the bias towards the Church of England which National Schools displayed. Such schools generally received support from the British and Foreign School Society, founded in 1808 by the Quaker Joseph Lancaster to promote non-denominational education. Halesowen's first British School, however, owed its origin to the philanthropy of one individual, Caleb Bloomer. Bloomer was the son of Thomas Bloomer, a nail ironmonger, who had a warehouse at Haywood Wharf, and lived at Haywood House, which stood south-east of the bridge carrying Mucklow Hill over the canal. Caleb Bloomer built what became known as Islington Ragged School on Stourbridge Road in 1867. As it had a baptistery at one end of the schoolroom, it was obviously designed to serve as a church as well as a school. Caleb Bloomer lived at nearby Beulah Lodge where he regularly entertained visiting preachers; he died in 1872 whilst on a trip to the Holy Land. Attached to his will was a document giving his executors instructions on how to continue his work at the Ragged School. One executor, however, refused to serve and Bloomer's brothers contested the provisions of the will.[4] The school closed down but was later purchased by the Primitive Methodists, possibly for a place of worship, but more likely as a school. The 1876 *Directory* shows that the Ragged School, with Miss Emma Higgs as Mistress, was still in existence.

116 *Stourbridge Road County Primary School, 1966.*

Perhaps in response to the Education Act of 1870, the Congregational Church at Great Cornbow appointed Samuel Mawer and his wife as Master and Mistress to run a day school. It had an average attendance of 120 pupils by 1873 and was described as a British School in the *Directory* of 1876, when the Master was Archibald Hindle and the Mistress, Sarah Ann Jones. In 1878 this school, having outgrown the accommodation at Great Cornbow, amalgamated with the Ragged School on Stourbridge Road. A board of trustees was formed and the name was changed to the British School. By 1884 it had an average attendance of 350 children. In 1901, a large extension provided space for an extra 250 children. With County Councils taking over responsibility for elementary education under the Education Act of 1902, Worcestershire County Council negotiated the purchase of the British School from the trustees; the sale went through in 1905 and the school became one of several county elementary schools in the town.

Board Schools

The promoters of the 1870 Education Act sought to ensure that every child would receive an elementary education. This was to be provided either by voluntary effort or by the establishment of an elected school board, supported by a local school rate. Neither the established Church nor the nonconformists in Halesowen liked the idea

117 *Tenter Street Council School, 1973.*

of a school rate, so each church group continued to raise money to support its own day schools; all of them struggled to meet Department of Education standards. Most of Halesowen's National and British schools retained their independence until the County Council took control in 1903, but at Cradley a School Board was formed as late as 1899, building new girls and infants schools at Colley Lane in 1902.

Council Schools

The 1902 Education Act gave control of education to County Councils and County Boroughs. From 1903, Worcestershire County Council was able to support the former National Schools, which were all renamed Church of England schools. It was also able to build new schools to serve a rapidly growing population in the

118   *Holt Lane Council School, c.1930.*

town. Holt Road School, Cakemore, was built in 1907 for 370 boys and girls and 250 infants, and Tenter Street School, Halesowen, was built in 1909 for 246 boys, 246 girls and 256 infants.[5] In another surge of school building the County Council built Olive Hill Council School in 1938 for 450 pupils, and Priory Road School, Lapal, for 343 children.

Secondary Modern Schools

Worcestershire County Council also promoted secondary schools in Halesowen. Hill and Cakemore County Modern Boys School, Long Lane, was built in 1928 for 360 boys, and Hill and Cakemore County Modern Girls School, Long Lane, was built in the same year for 400 girls. The County Modern Boys School in

119   *County Modern Boys School, Stourbridge Road, 1966.*

120   *County Modern Girls School, Bundle Hill, 1966.*

Stourbridge Road was built in 1939 for 300 boys; the Bundle Hill County Modern Girls School was built for 330 girls in the same year. The co-educational Cradley County Modern School was built at Homer Hill, also in 1939, for 453 boys and girls. These schools took children over the age of 11 out of the former elementary schools, which now became primary schools.

Technical Education

Even during the Victorian period the government was aware that industrial development in Germany and the United States was beginning to outstrip that of Great Britain. The Technical Education Act of 1889 enabled County Councils to establish technical, or science and art schools, in industrial districts. A Technical School with three classrooms was built in Old Hawne Lane in 1897. This later proved inadequate, and evening classes were held in several other buildings including the

Grammar School, Tenter Street Boys' School, the Church of England School, the Senior Boys' and Girls' Schools in Long Lane, and at Colley Lane Boys' School. The building was replaced by a new Technical School in 1939.

The County Technical School was built in Furnace Lane, near the Grammar School, and opened on 17 April 1939. It began as a Junior Day Technical and Commercial School, admitting boys and girls between 13 and 16 years of age. There were drawing offices and engineering workshops, cookery and needlework rooms on the ground floor, and a library, science laboratory, and woodwork, bookkeeping and typewriting rooms on the first floor. The school also offered part-time day and evening classes. The first Principal was Dr Johnson Ball, a noted antiquarian and author of the standard work on the locally born type-founder, William Caslon. The name was changed to Halesowen College of Further Education in 1960 to reflect the growing importance of Further Education in its work.[6] The building of the new

121 *The former Technical School, Old Hawne Lane, 1966.*

122 *Halesowen Technical School, 1962.*

College of Further Education at Whittingham Road in 1966 should have enabled the Secondary Technical School to re-emerge, but, to facilitate the introduction of comprehensive education, the Technical School amalgamated with the Grammar School in 1966. The combined school became comprehensive in 1972, and was renamed the Earls High School.

Comprehensive School

By 1971, there were 5,317 children at the 20 primary schools in Halesowen. The Grammar School had 950 pupils, whilst a further 2,163 children attended the five secondary modern schools in the borough. All this was to change in 1972 with the implementation of Worcestershire County Council's plan for comprehensive schooling. This involved not only the abolition of the 'eleven-plus', but also a move to a three-tier system of first, middle and secondary schools. The Earls High School became a mixed comprehensive school for 13- to 18-year-olds. The County Secondary Modern Boys School, Stourbridge Road, was renamed the Richmond High School, and the County Modern Girls School, Bundle Hill, became the Walton High School, both single-sex comprehensive schools catering for 13- to 18-year-olds. The Secondary Modern schools at Hill and Cakemore amalgamated to form the Leasowes High School. This was housed in the former boys` school building, whilst the girls' school next door became Greenhill Middle School. The remaining Secondary Modern school at Cradley also became a middle school, taking children from nine to 13 years of age. These changes were complete before Local Government Re-organisation took effect in April 1974, from which date Dudley Metropolitan Borough became the education authority.

123 *The Leasowes High School, Long Lane, 1974.*

By the 1980s many education authorities were abandoning the middle schools experiment and centralising post-16 tuition in sixth-form colleges. Dudley Metropolitan Borough adopted this policy in 1982. The Earls High School and Halesowen's other comprehensive schools now catered for 11- to 16-year-olds, gaining younger pupils, but losing their sixth formers. Richmond High School and Walton High School amalgamated on the Stourbridge Road site to form a mixed comprehensive called the Windsor High School. The former girls' school at Bundle Hill became the Walton Campus of an enlarged Halesowen College of Further Education, which now took over the education of Halesowen's 16- to 18-year-olds. Cradley's former Secondary Modern School at Homer Hill, which had been a middle school for ten years, also became a comprehensive, Cradley High School. The Leasowes High School continued at Long Lane until moving to new buildings on Kent Road in 1987. It was then renamed the Leasowes Community College. By 2000, Halesowen had four mixed comprehensive schools, the largest being Windsor High School with 1,360 pupils. Leasowes Community College had 1,180 students, The Earls High School 1,170 students and Cradley High School, 730 students.

Halesowen College of Further Education

When Halesowen Technical School was absorbed into the Grammar School in 1966, many of its courses were continued at the new Halesowen College of Further Education, Whittingham Road. The college was officially opened on 23 June 1967. The architects were Richard Sheppard, Robson & Partners, London, and the building cost £231,500 plus £62,000 for furniture and equipment. At the 1982 reorganisation of post-16 education in the south of Dudley Metropolitan Borough, the College of Further Education was renamed Halesowen College and became a tertiary college offering 'A' Level courses to all the town's 16- to 18-year-olds. The number of enrolments at the college increased throughout the 1980s and the College took over the former Walton High School, Bundle Hill. By 2000, the College had 11,000 enrolments per year, 42 per cent of them for 16- to 18-year-olds. The Walton Campus, as it became known, continued in use until the centralisation of all facilities at Whittingham Road in 2003. The former County Secondary Modern School for Girls, an important local landmark, was then demolished.

Chapter IX

LOCAL GOVERNMENT

The origins of local government in Halesowen can be traced back to a grant made about 1270 by Henry III to the Abbot of Hales to create a borough there. The original document no longer survives but there is a contemporary copy amongst the Lyttelton papers:

> To all Christ's faithful people to whom the present writing shall come Brother E. ... by divine permission the humble minister of Hales and the Convent of the same place in the name of the Lord greetings. Be it known to all that King Henry for the safety of his own soul and the souls of his predecessors and successors has granted to us licence to make a Borough of Hales with all liberties and free customs appertaining to boroughs; and that henceforth all who after this Royal concession shall receive burgages in the Borough of Hales from us shall enjoy their possessions freely quietly and in peace rendering to us annually for each burgage twelve pence for all services at two times agreeable to us, namely at the Feast of St Michael sixpence and at the Feast of Easter sixpence; we are willing and grant that the burgages of the Borough of Hales shall have all the liberties and free customs which the burgesses of Hereford have, which the aforesaid burgesses of Hales themselves have chosen to observe; we also grant common of pasture throughout our Manor of Hales and where all men of our Manor have had pasture without our defended domains and closes, and also pastures and closes to the water-courses in the wood which extends from our new mill to the ford at Chatley; and therefore that our grant may remain permanent and established we have strengthened it by this present writing and by the Authority of our Seal, these being witnesses: Dom E. Abbott of Welebecke; Thomas and Philip, chaplains of Hales; Dom. Richard, son of Wiliam; Richard de Bulay; Simon de Frankeley; Henry de Hamstede; Richard, clerk.[1]

It is significant that this grant was made to the Abbot of Hales and not to the burgesses of Halesowen. Burgesses in a town paid a nominal annual rent for their plots of land, or 'burgages', and were free from the duty of cultivating the land of the lord of the manor with which copyhold tenants in a village were burdened. The older deeds of properties in High Street and Peckingham Street refer to burgages, but the regularly spaced building plots on the southern side of Great Cornbow are the best examples and suggest that this area was deliberately planned to attract incoming businessmen who might contribute to the economic success of the new borough. The field behind Great Cornbow, now cut in two by Queensway, was called 'Burgidge' on the 1844 tithe map.

Apart from the extra rental the Abbot could expect to gain from the burgage plots, he could also anticipate increased tolls at the local market and a regular income from fines in the borough court, which he established to keep the burgesses under control. There is no evidence that Halesowen ever sent representatives to Parliament, so it seems likely that successive abbots gave the Halesowen burgesses very limited freedoms, probably allowing them some influence on the numbers admitted to particular trades. Newcomers, however, still had to purchase the right to trade in Halesowen from the Abbot rather than the burgesses. In many towns where lords of the manor set up boroughs as speculations, they later relinquished control and gave the burgesses their independence in return for a significant payment. This did not happen in Halesowen where the landlord was an Abbot who regarded his powers as a sacred inheritance which was not to be dissipated. By the time the abbey was dissolved, there was no dynamic in the town for independence, although Sir John Dudley did build a new market house in 1539.[2] The officials of the borough continued to be elected annually at the lord of the manor's borough court, presumably held in the market house. By the late 18th century these officials included a bailiff and sub-bailiff, a constable, an ale taster, two searchers and sealers of leather and two overseers of swine.

Highways

An Act of Parliament of 1555 made all parishes responsible for the repair of highways. Surveyors were to be appointed annually by the overseers to ensure that all parishioners, or their substitutes, spent four days per year mending the roads. A further Act of 1563 increased the number of days' work to six and made justices of the peace responsible for ensuring that each parish fulfilled its obligations. This duty would have fallen heavily on Halesowen which had to maintain several miles of the great road from Bromsgrove to Dudley and, too, the desperately steep road out of the town towards Birmingham. In 1679 John Hadley of Halesowen, a nailer, aged 45, testified at an enquiry into the state of local bridges that he was 'compelled by the overseer within the parish … to take his tumbrel and horses to carry cinders and gravel from a furnace and waterfall within the said parish of Halesowen to repair and mend the highways in the said parish'. There was some argument as to whether borough and parish should co-operate in the repair of each other's roads and bridges. The 1679 enquiry took evidence on the poor state of the bridges next to the blade mill at Cornbow and the malt mill at the bottom of Mucklow Hill. All agreed that bridges were maintained either by the borough or the parish, but several local inhabitants, including Edward Paston, the ejected Commonwealth minister, complained that the lord of the manor should have repaired these wooden bridges, which had only replaced ancient fords after he had deepened the channels at the two mills. One of those giving evidence, William Grove, of Hawn, a nailer, aged 57, had

> been head overseer of the whole parish which does extend as well to the Borough as the parish and at that time did mend or pay for the mending of a bridge that lies in the Borough

called Stonebowe Bridge and this deponent conceives that when he was overseer as aforesaid he had power to cause the ways in the Borough to be repaired and that if any inhabitants of the Borough refused so to do that he could compel them thereunto.[3]

The creation of turnpike roads in the 18th century (see Chapter 4, p.90) relieved the surveyors of highways of responsibility for maintaining the major roads through their parishes, but the system of requiring parishioners to help repair minor roads continued.

The Poor Law

During the 16th and 17th centuries, national legislation began to impinge more on the daily lives of Halesowen residents. An Act of 1572 enabled parishes to appoint officials to collect donations for the poor. These 'overseers of the poor' were 'from 1597' able to collect poor rates and 'after 1601' to erect workhouses where the poor could be put to work. There was perhaps little need for a workhouse in Halesowen, as the iron trade was expanding so rapidly that there would be little unemployment, and the churchwardens owned several cottages near the church which could accommodate poor widows. It wasn't until 1730 that Sir Thomas Lyttelton gave land at the far end of Church Street for a parish workhouse, by which time such institutions actually gave shelter as well as employment.[4]

Municipal Corporations Act, 1835

In the 19th century, central government tried to ensure that all boroughs held elections and that all ratepayers had a vote. Commissioners were sent out to discover the origins and constitutions of hundreds of English boroughs. In not inviting the commissioners to Halesowen, the town's leaders committed a fatal error and the town was omitted from the schedule of boroughs appended to the Municipal Corporations Act of 1835. Perhaps the Lyttelton family did not wish to produce Halesowen's ancient charter and expose their control of the town to outside scrutiny. The result was that when decisions were subsequently made about the formation of the new poor law unions, Halesowen had no official status beyond that of a rural parish, and was divided amongst its more powerful neighbours.

The Parish of Halesowen

Until 1834, the ancient parish of Halesowen, covering 12,272 acres, included Halesowen Borough and the hamlets of Romsley, Hunnington, Illey, Lapal, Hasbury, Hawne, Hill, Cakemore, Ridgacre, Oldbury and part of Warley, which were in Shropshire, along with Cradley, Lutley and the remainder of Warley, which were in Worcestershire. The manor of Halesowen was, however, smaller. Oldbury had been made a separate manor by Robert Dudley in 1557 and had developed into a town with a larger population than that of Halesowen. In 1834 the lord of the manor of Oldbury was Francis Parrot of Hawkesbury, near Coventry. Cradley, too, was a separate manor, although it was held by the Lyttelton family, lords of the manor of

Halesowen. Lutley manor had always belonged to the College of Wolverhampton, but this was dissolved by the Wolverhampton Rectory Act of 1848.

Population, 1841

Halesowen Borough	2,056
Cakemore	357
Cradley	2,686
Hasbury	919
Hawne	110
Hill	936
Hunnington	158
Illey	94
Lapal	351
Lutley	137
Oldbury	7,374
Ridgacre	465
Romsley	413
Warley Salop	356
Warley Wigorn	964
Total of Halesowen Parish	17,376

124 *Walter Somers, first Chairman of Halesowen Rural District Council, 1894.*

Until 1832 most of the Halesowen residents who met the property qualification, and could therefore vote in Parliamentary elections, voted for a candidate to represent Shropshire. The voters of Cradley, Lutley and Warley Wigorn, however, voted for a Worcestershire Member of Parliament. This anomaly was corrected by the Parliamentary Boundaries Act of 1832, which, for parliamentary purposes, placed the whole of the ancient parish of Halesowen in Worcestershire. The jurisdiction of Shropshire Justices of the Peace over parts of the parish was in turn curtailed by the Counties (Detached Parts) Act of 1844, which returned the Shropshire parts of Halesowen to Worcestershire after nearly 800 years.

The Poor Law Amendment Act, 1834

The ancient parish of Halesowen, with its 14 hamlets in two counties, did not suit the bureaucrats who formulated the Poor Law Amendment Act of 1834. Under this measure parishes were joined into large units to deal with the growing numbers claiming poor relief. Most of the parish of Halesowen, including the borough, was put into the Stourbridge Poor Law Union. The inmates of Halesowen's small workhouse in Church Street were moved to the new Stourbridge Union Workhouse at Wordsley. Oldbury, however, along with Warley Salop and Warley Wigorn, was joined to West Bromwich Poor Law Union; Romsley and Hunnington were allocated to the Bromsgrove Union. At a stroke, Halesowen lost control of half its population and became a poor relation of its long-term commercial rival, Stourbridge.

Halesowen Poor in 1884[5]

Hamlet	Numbers in Stourbridge Union Workhouse	Expenditure on outdoor relief £
Halesowen Borough	22	257
Cakemore	8	20
Cradley	26	329
Hasbury	9	142
Hawne	3	22
Hill	5	180
Illey	0	19
Lapal	1	31
Lutley	0	16
Ridgacre	3	42
	77	1,058

The 1834 Poor Law Union boundaries were followed as central government gave more responsibilities to local government. The Public Health Act of 1875 led to the formation of Urban and Rural Sanitary Authorities whose responsibility it was to appoint medical officers and provide sewage, water and waste services. Stourbridge, which already had a Board of Improvement Commissioners, became an Urban Sanitary Authority, whilst the remainder of the Union, including Halesowen, became the Stourbridge Rural Sanitary Authority.

The Police Force

During the 19th century, it became increasingly obvious that parish constables could no longer be expected to maintain law and order in growing industrial towns. It might become the turn of any respectable citizen to be constable for a year, dealing with paupers and vagrants, and using his power of citizen's arrest to apprehend more serious wrong-doers to come before the Justices of the Peace in Quarter Sessions. The work was onerous and unpaid. Wealthier citizens employed a substitute to do the job for them. Kidderminster was one of the first local towns to recognise the inadequacy of this system and, from 1823, to employ a team of night watchmen instead. In 1839, the Court of Quarter Sessions at Worcester formed a Police Committee and appointed a Chief Constable to build up a county police force. It is not clear when Halesowen's first police station was opened, but the *Directory* of 1842 gave its location as Church Street. In 1847 a new police station, with cells adjoining, was built in Great Cornbow by the County and District Constables Committee. The imposing building had large transomed mullioned windows either side of the entrance, and three Dutch gables on the first floor facing Great Cornbow. The first Superintendent, Miles Overend, lived in an elegant two-storey house attached to the west end of the police station. In 1881, the Superintendent was Henry Kemp. By 1899, the original station was deemed inadequate, and a replacement building was opened on New Road, near the Grammar School. The old building in Cornbow was then sold to Halesowen Rural District Council for use as council offices.[6]

125 *The former police station, Great Cornbow, 1957. After the opening of the new police station in New Road in 1889 the building was used as offices by Halesowen Rural District Council. Part of the structure was demolished in 1930 and the public conveniences were built in its place.*

Worcestershire County Council

The Local Government Act of 1888 extended to counties the principle of democratic elections, which had been imposed on boroughs in 1835. The non-elected Justices of the Peace in Quarter Sessions, who had ruled the counties since medieval times, were replaced by elected county councillors, who began their deliberations in 1889. Their chief responsibilities were the control of the police force and the maintenance of main roads and county bridges. From 1903, county councils took control of education, enabling them to assist such long-established schools as Halesowen Grammar School, and to bring together National and British schools. The Local Government Act of 1929 greatly added to the work of county councils by abolishing the separate Poor Law Unions and giving control of poor relief to county public assistance committees. The workhouses were no longer the dreaded last resort of the destitute and became centres for the care of the elderly and infirm.

Worcestershire County Council's main contribution to the Halesowen landscape was the building of primary and secondary schools after 1903 (see Chapter 6, pp.138-9) and the construction of the Halesowen bypass, which opened in 1958. The County Council continued to provide strategic services in the Halesowen area until local government reorganisation in 1974, when all its powers over the town passed to Dudley Metropolitan Borough.

Halesowen Rural District Council

The Local Government Act of 1894, gave the Rural Sanitary Authority new powers and a new name; Halesowen Rural District Council was formed, including Lye and Wollescote until 1897, and Quinton until 1910. The duties of the newly elected councillors were to include sanitation and sewage, local roads and, eventually, housing. At first, the Rural District Council met at the Public Offices, 26 Great Cornbow, which belonged to the solicitors, Homfray and Goodman. When Worcestershire

County Council built a new police station in New Road in 1899, the Council bought the redundant station in the centre of Great Cornbow, holding their first meeting in the new Council Chamber there on 6 February 1901. This building, sometimes called the New Public Offices, was in turn closed in 1933 with the opening of the new library and Council Chamber in Hagley Street. Most of the former police station was then demolished and replaced by the public conveniences. The remaining parts, including the fire station, remained in use until the late 1950s.

Halesowen Urban District Council

In 1924 the true character of the town was recognised when Halesowen became an Urban District Council with enhanced powers. The council area was

126   *The Old Public Offices, 26 Great Cornbow, 1973.*

divided into seven wards: Cradley Ward was represented by four councillors; Hill Ward had three councillors; Halesowen, Hasbury and Cakemore Wards each had two; Hawne and Lapal wards had one councillor each. In 1927, the Council

127   *Council House, Great Cornbow, purchased by Halesowen Urban District Council in 1927.*

purchased the big house at 25 Great Cornbow which had formerly been the home of John Wright, solicitor. Council offices were centralised in the building and a new Council Chamber and public library were built on the land behind in 1933. Branch libraries were opened at Cradley and Long Lane in 1936.

The most obvious achievement of the Rural and Urban District Councils was in the area of public housing; using powers given by the 1919 and subsequent Housing Acts, the Councils had built 994 houses by 1936, and a further 288 were under construction. The Councils had also subsidised the erection of 514 houses by private builders under the Housing Act of 1923. Another significant development

128   *Halesowen Central Library, built in 1933.*

was the Urban District Council's purchase of the 123-acre Leasowes Estate in 1934. Part of the grounds was already leased to Halesowen Golf Club, but the remainder became a public park. The walled garden there became a nursery for plants for other parks within the town, including the recreation ground at Highfield Lane and the gardens at the Finger Post. Part of the disused section of the Dudley Canal between Mucklow Hill and Manor Lane was purchased and added to the Leasowes.

Halesowen Borough Council

The next stage in Halesowen's development as a local authority was the winning of borough status in 1936. As a municipal borough, Halesowen gained few powers that it didn't already enjoy as an urban district, but securing a new borough charter, and the right to have a mayor rather than a chairman, was seen as a great boost to civic pride. There were three councillors elected for each of five wards: Central,

129 *The Council Chamber, 1933.*

130 *Halesowen Central Library interior, 1933.*

North, South, East and West. The first mayor, chosen because of the number of years he had served on the Council, was John Benjamin Downing.[7]

The new Borough Council built 906 houses between 1936 and the outbreak of the Second World War. In the same period, the Council issued 405 demolition and closure orders. After the war, the Borough Council developed the Hasbury Farm, Fatherless Barn and Howley Grange estates. The Council also built the controversial Highfield flats in Halesowen, with 255 dwellings first occupied in 1964, and the unfortunate Tanhouse Lane flats, Cradley, where the 535 dwellings were opened in 1969 only to be demolished 30 years later. In all, the Borough Council built 3,491 houses between 1945 and 1971; 4,400 houses were erected by private builders in the same period. During the 1950s, the Council purchased and demolished many old cottages in Islington, Little Cornbow, Birmingham Street and Brook Road. A notable purchase was the site of the former *Cross Guns Inn*, 43 Birmingham Street, bought for £130 from Edward Byng in 1954. Between 1945 and 1971, the Council issued 1,214 demolition and closure orders.[8]

A notable achievement of Halesowen Borough Council was the building of the public swimming baths, which opened in July 1963; the pool was built to Amateur Swimming Association Standards and is 110 feet long. The project was a particular crusade of Halesowen's longest serving councillor, and three times mayor, Walter Hodgetts, who served as an Independent, believing that local councils should not divide on party lines. It was unfortunate that the decision to build the baths near the

131 *Council houses, St John's Road, 1957.*

Council House led to the demolition of 19 and 20 Great Cornbow, which were amongst the town's most significant buildings of special architectural or historic interest.

The Conservative Club

The Conservative Club was started in about 1896 in premises on Hagley Street next to Lloyds Bank. Benjamin Cockin was the first manager, and his wife, Mary, succeeded him in the post. By 1904, the Conservative Club had moved to Cross House, the big house next to the *Star Inn* at the top of Peckingham Street. The 1907 architect's drawing for the repair of these buildings shows the word 'club' on a plaque on the wall between the big arched windows. By 1912, the Halesowen & District Conservative & Unionist Club had moved to Stourbridge Road, occupying the white building facing Church Street, formerly known as Townsend House. This

132 *Council flats, Kent Road, 1952.*

Population

Halesowen Rural District

1901 22,611
1911 25,765
1921 28,382

Halesowen Urban District

1931 30,350

Halesowen Borough

1951 39,884
1961 44,160
1971 53,990

133 *Swimming Pool, Great Cornbow, opened in 1963.*

134 *Private houses built by A. & J. Mucklow & Co. Ltd at Briery Road, Hasbury, 1957.*

had been the home of Edward Moore, surgeon, to whose memory there is a stained glass window in St John's Church. It had also been occupied by other doctors, including Hugh Richard Ker and Joseph Arthur Arkwright. The Conservative Club remained in these premises until they were demolished in 1973 to build the traffic island.

135   *Conservative Club, Stourbridge Road, 1967.*

The Liberal Club

The first Liberal Club was opened in about 1896 in premises in Great Cornbow, near the corner of Hagley Street, where J.H. Hobbs' hardware shop now stands. In 1906 the Club had moved to the big house on the corner of Hagley Street and Laurel Lane; this had been purchased for £900 from the trustees of William Russell, carrier, who had run a daily cart service to Birmingham. The trustees of the Halesowen & District Liberal Association at this time were:

William Green of Webb's Green, farmer
Joseph Hackett of Hasbury, farmer
Thomas Crumpton of Halesowen, contractor
Aaron Oliver of Halesowen, carpenter
Edwin Partridge of Halesowen, bolt manufacturer
Elijah Timmins of Halesowen, builder
George Crumpton of Halesowen, retired carpenter
Harry Jones of Halesowen, boot dealer
William Price the younger of Hasbury, miner
Alfred Hackett of Hasbury, night soil contractor
Thomas Edward Rose of Halesowen, carpenter
Joseph Seeley of Halesowen, warehouseman
John Jones of Halesowen, carpenter
William Shilvock of Halesowen, boot manufacturer
Thomas Pearman of Lutley, farmer
Charles Parish of Hasbury, rate collector
Henry Beard of Halesowen, road foreman
John Dancer of Halesowen, boot dealer

The Liberal Club remained in the Hagley Street premises until about 1978 when they were demolished for the building of a supermarket.

136 *Liberal Club, Hagley Street, 1962.*

The Labour Club

The Halesowen and Hasbury Labour Club occupied rooms at the back of the Co-operative confectionery shop at 34 Hagley Street. In 1951, the Chairman was J. Hickton and the Secretary was H. Male. When the Co-operative shop was rebuilt in 1962, the Labour Club moved to a new building at 52 Hagley Road.

The West Midlands Special Review Area

A serious threat to Halesowen's independent existence came in 1960 with the report of the Local Government Commission on the West Midlands Special Review Area. It was proposed that 13 urban districts and municipal boroughs, in the area popularly known as the Black Country, should be absorbed by the County Boroughs of Dudley, Smethwick, West Bromwich, Walsall and Wolverhampton. Halesowen was to join Oldbury and Rowley Regis in an enlarged Smethwick County Borough. The report provoked a furious dispute within Halesowen Borough Council with the Labour members supporting the proposed amalgamation and the Conservatives and Liberals combining to oppose it. Alderman Clifford Willetts, however, who had been the first Labour mayor in 1950, backed the independence campaign and was expelled from the Labour Party. A Halesowen Independence Committee was formed and held a postal vote on the issue: 65 per cent of the electorate voted, with 20,957 voting for Halesowen's independence as a borough within Worcestershire and only 242 voting for amalgamation with Smethwick, Oldbury and Rowley Regis. With the support of the County Council, Halesowen made the dubious claim that it was more a Worcestershire market town than an integral part of the Black Country.

Whilst the government's decision was awaited, the term of Miss E.M. Bridge as mayor of Halesowen was coming to an end. The Labour Party nominee to be the next mayor, Councillor Ashley Neale, had supported amalgamation. After a heated debate

137 *John Benjamin Downing, the first mayor of Halesowen, 1936.*

138 *Clifford Willetts, the first Labour mayor of Halesowen, 1950.*

139 *William Parkes, mayor of Halesowen, 1951.*

he was not invited to take office, breaking a gentleman's agreement that the next most senior councillor became mayor. Miss Bridge, a Conservative, and Halesowen's first female Mayor, continued for a second year. In the event the independence campaign was successful, and amalgamation with neighbouring towns was postponed.

Local Government Reorganisation

Successive governments were still keen to create fewer, and more effective, local authorities. In 1966, Harold Wilson's Labour government appointed Lord Redcliffe-Maud to chair a Royal Commission on Local Government in England. In his report of 1969 Redcliffe-Maud argued that small local government areas could not afford to provide the range of services which people then expected of them. His new local government areas would have higher numbers of rate payers and would be able to make economies of scale in delivering services. His proposals, modified by Edward Heath's Conservative government, were made law by the Local Government Act of 1972. Halesowen and Stourbridge were to merge with Dudley to form Dudley Metropolitan District with a population of 294,000. Not only were the two towns to lose their separate councils, but they were to be moved out of Worcestershire into a new strategic authority, West Midlands County Council, stretching from Wolverhampton in the north west to Coventry in the south east, with a combined population of 2,790,000. The new authorities came into being in April 1974. Although Margaret Thatcher's government abolished West Midlands County Council along with the other Metropolitan County Councils in 1986, Dudley Metropolitan Borough has endured for 30 years.

Of the 72 members of Dudley Council, only 12 represent Halesowen wards. Even if they were to unite on a local issue, they could easily be overruled by

140 *Leonard Harper, mayor of Halesowen, 1953.*

141 *Edith Maud Bridge, mayor of Halesowen, 1960.*

142 *Walter Hodgetts, mayor of Halesowen in 1940, 1941 and 1962.*

143 *Halesowen Borough Council, 1962.*

whichever political group held power in Council. The desire of Halesowen and Stourbridge to retain some separate identity was met by the creation of township councils. Halesowen Township Council was established in 1979 with the objective of obtaining parish council status, but Dudley Metropolitan Borough Council has never encouraged such moves. These township councils have no statutory authority and they have been singularly ineffective in giving each town a strong voice in Dudley. As recently as 1996, at a Civic Service marking the 60th anniversary of the granting of Halesowen's borough charter, the rector of Halesowen, Canon John Everest, spoke out in favour of 'a democratically elected, accountable forum to bring together local people to discuss local issues'. His words are still valid today, when even the Halesowen Township Council is in abeyance.

Chairmen and Mayors of Halesowen Rural District, Urban District and Borough Councils 1894-1974

Rural District Council

1894	Walter Somers, Belle Vue House, forge master
1895	Walter Somers, Belle Vue House, forge master
1896	Walter Somers, Belle Vue House, forge master
1897	Walter Somers, Belle Vue House, forge master
1898	William Green, Webb's Green, farmer
1899	Charles Hodgetts Clewes, Park Road, Cradley, rope manufacturer
1900	Arthur James Grove, Bloomfield House, Stourbridge Road, button manufacturer
1901	Arthur James Grove, Bloomfield House, Stourbridge Road, button manufacturer
1902	George Benjamin Parkes, Haywood House, Mucklow Hill, iron founder
1903	Thomas Hodgetts, Summer Hill, postmaster
1904	William Green, Webb's Green, farmer
1905	George Hadley, Merton Villa, Cakemore, confectioner
1906	Benjamin Marsland, 14 Waxland Road, Manager of Halesowen & Hasbury Co-op. Society
1907	Frank Hipkiss, Woodlands, Windmill Hill, Cradley, anchor manufacturer
1908	Frank Hipkiss, Woodlands, Windmill Hill, Cradley, anchor manufacturer
1909	John Bloomer, Hasbury, farmer
1910	Benjamin Marsland, 14 Waxland Road, Manager of Halesowen & Hasbury Co-op. Society
1911	Benjamin Marsland, 14 Waxland Road, Manager of Halesowen & Hasbury Co-op. Society
1912	Benjamin Southall, West Road, Cradley, grocer
1913	George Benjamin Parkes, Haywood House, Mucklow Hill, iron founder
1914	George Benjamin Parkes, Haywood House, Mucklow Hill, iron founder
1915	John Benjamin Downing, 76 Attwood Street, beer retailer
1916	James Areli Tate, Woodlands, Quarry Lane, Hasbury, farmer
1917	Thomas Hodgetts, Summer Hill, postmaster
1918	Joseph Parsons, 22 Cobham Road, foreman, Stewarts & Lloyds
1919	Joseph Parsons, 22 Cobham Road, foreman, Stewarts & Lloyds
1920	Frank Hipkiss, Woodlands, Windmill Hill, Cradley, anchor manufacturer
1921	William Green, Webb's Green, farmer (son of former chairman)
1922	Herbert John Cox, Holloway House, Drew's Holloway, ironmonger
1923	John Benjamin Downing, Ivy House, Church Street, iron merchant
1924	Henry Reece, Lynton House, Drew's Holloway, chain manufacturer

Urban District Council

1925	John Chapman, Eastbourne, Dudley Road, Halesowen, mining engineer
1926	Eli Beard, Broseley, Waxland Road
1927	John Benjamin Downing, Ivy House, Church Street, iron merchant
1928	Richard Green, Colley Gate House, Cradley, chain manufacturer
1929	Joseph Parsons, 22 Cobham Road, foreman, Stewarts & Lloyds
1930	William Green, Webb's Green, farmer
1931	Edward Charles Starling, Colley Gate, Cradley, grocer

1932   Charles Henry Head, *Samson & Lion*, Alexandra Road
1933   Herbert John Cox, Holloway House, Drew's Holloway, ironmonger
1934   John Benjamin Downing, Ivy House, Church Street, iron merchant
1935   Walter Hodgetts, 11 Ladysmith Road, Cradley, schoolteacher
1936   Thomas Smith, Minstead, Mucklow Hill, Halesowen

Borough Council

1936   John Benjamin Downing, Ivy House, Church Street, iron merchant
1937   John Benjamin Downing, Ivy House, Church Street, iron merchant
1938   Herbert John Cox, Holloway House, Drew's Holloway, ironmonger
1939   Herbert John Cox, Holloway House, Drew's Holloway, ironmonger
1940   Walter Hodgetts, Walizmur, Colley Lane, Cradley, schoolteacher
1941   Walter Hodgetts, Walizmur, Colley Lane, Cradley, schoolteacher
1942   Thomas Smith, Minstead, Mucklow Hill, nut and bolt manufacturer
1943   Thomas Smith, Minstead, Mucklow Hill, nut and bolt manufacturer
1944   Herbert Parkes, Lower Friars House, Worcester Road, Harvington, builder
1945   Herbert Parkes, Lower Friars House, Worcester Road, Harvington, builder
1946   Francis Lionel Rose, Ind., Wheatfields, Bromsgrove Road, Hunnington, tube manufacturer
1947   Francis Lionel Rose, Ind., Wheatfields, Bromsgrove Road, Hunnington, tube manufacturer
1948   Francis Lionel Rose, Ind., Wheatfields, Bromsgrove Road, Hunnington, tube manufacturer
1949   Alfred George Rudge, Ind., Waxland Road, solicitor
1950   Clifford Willetts, Lab., 46 Clent View Road, Cradley, chain striker
1951   William Parkes, Lib., 20 Masters Lane, Blackheath, builder
1952   John Henry Green, Ind. 63, Hill Street, Hasbury
1953   Leonard Harper, Con., Highbury, Bromsgrove Road, Hunnington, builder
1954   George Albert Southall, Lab., 8 Witley Avenue, caterer
1955   Albert Henry Spring, Con., 32 Astley Avenue, Quinton
1956   Philip Timmins, Ind., Avondale, Shelton Lane, Cradley, estate agent
1957   Peter Ward Scott, Con., 107 Spies Lane, Quinton, demolition contractor
1958   Norman Garner, Lib., 21 Masters Lane, Blackheath, *Grand Hotel*, Birmingham
1959   Harry Davies, Con., 51 Gower Road, Quinton, company director
1960   Elsie Maud Bridge, Con., 53 Grange Road, director, Hackett Bros.
1961   Elsie Maud Bridge Con., 53 Grange Road, director, Hackett Bros.
1962   Walter Hodgetts, Ind., Walizmur, Colley Lane, Cradley, schoolteacher
1963   David Charles Herbert, Lab., 25 Richmond Street, employed at Stewarts & Lloyds
1964   Albert Whitehouse, Lib., Colley Gate, builder
1965   Richard Blakeway, Lib., 28 Hillwood Road
1966   Robert John Bird, Lib., 29 Colley Lane, Cradley, telephone engineer
1967   Norman Garner, Lib., 21 Masters Lane, Blackheath, *Grand Hotel*, Birmingham
1968   Kenneth Wilmore Johnson, Con., 36 Raddens Road, company director
1969   Albert Brodie, Con., 16 Long Lane, police sergeant
1970   William Cedric John Ray, Con., 31 St Kenelm's Avenue, caterer
1971   Arthur Norman Brown, Lab., 47 Stourbridge Road, postman
1972   Catherine Graham, Con., 15 Long Lane
1973   Frank Price, Lab., 66 Alexandra Road

Chapter X

THE REDEVELOPMENT OF HALESOWEN

ॐ॰ॐ

After the Second World War, Halesowen Borough Council developed a plan for the comprehensive redevelopment of the town centre. The Council acknowledged that theirs was an ambitious project and that it would involve 'the removal of the majority of the existing properties'. The mayor's Christmas card of 1948 had an artist's impression of the new town with a new street forming a junction with Hagley Street opposite Great Cornbow. With prominent builders on the council, including Herbert Parkes, William Parkes and Leonard Harper, it was natural that there was a presumption in favour of rebuilding rather than renovating the town's shopping centre. The demolition contractor, Peter William Scott, who was mayor in 1957, may have been even more influential.

During the 1950s land at the rear of shops on High Street and Hagley Street was gradually purchased by the Council. In 1955, Sidney Shacklock, who ran a haberdasher's shop at 16 Church Street, accepted £1,350 for the old cottages called Gaunt's Yard, which overlooked the churchyard. In 1956 he sold 17 and 18 Church Street and in 1958 sold his own shop for £2,500. Wrenson's Stores Ltd sold the land behind their grocery shop at 4 High Street in 1958.[1] W.S. Welch & Son Ltd. sold the land to the rear of their drapery shop at 1 High Street to the Council in 1960; their shop was sold to City and Central Shops (Halesowen) Ltd in 1961 and Fine Fare, Halesowen's first supermarket, was built on the site.[2] With the purchase and demolition of Church Steps House in 1963, the Council was able to lay out Queensway, the road which was to encircle the new shopping centre. The first buildings to go up on Queensway

144 *Peter William Scott, demolition contractor, Mayor of Halesowen in 1957.*

162

145 *Post Office, Queensway, 1964.*

146 *New shops, Queensway, 1964.*

were a new post office and a row of six shops facing north towards the churchyard. These were opened in 1962.

The Halesowen development plan also involved the construction of flats on land north-west of Queensway, which until 1956 had been part of Highfields Park. The architects of these flats, Remo and Mary Grinelli and Miall Rhys-Davies, won a competition organised by the Borough Council and the Royal Institute of British Architects. The Highfield flats were completed in 1964, and were renovated in 1989. Highfields House, which had been occupied by the Rev. Colvile in preference to the Rectory in Church Street, was purchased by the Council in 1944 and itself converted into flats.[3] Highfields House was demolished in about 1965.

The opening of the Halesowen Bypass in 1958, linking Manor Lane to the Hagley Road at Hayley Green, took the bulk of through-traffic out of Hagley Street. This was a prerequisite of any rebuilding in the town centre. In February 1962, a model of the new central area was put on display at the Central Library.

147   *Architect's impression of The Precinct, about 1965*

148   *The Precinct from Hagley Street, 1973.*

In December 1963 Halesowen Borough Council gave outline planning permission for the construction of a large complex of shops, flats, car park and offices between Hagley Street and Queensway. On 25 November 1964, the Council entered into an agreement with the developers, City and Central Shops (Halesowen) Ltd, who were given a 99-year lease on the land. Final planning permission was granted in August 1965. The development company's architects were Bernard Engle & Partners, who were then, and still are, at the forefront of shopping centre design. The contractors were Token Construction Co. Ltd.

The completed shopping centre comprised 47 shop units laid out on either side of a walkway from Hagley Street, and a covered market and a Sainsbury's supermarket either side of an open square at the far end. Some measure of protection from the weather was afforded by the concrete canopies which extended over each shop

149   *Sainsbury's supermarket, The Precinct, 1969.*

front. A complex of ramps and stairs gave access from the square to 23 shops which opened onto Queensway, and to a circular restaurant called the 'Silver Dragon', which was raised up to first-floor level on four concrete columns. A multi-storey car park for 400 cars was sited behind Sainsbury's store. The 'Precinct', as it was unimaginatively called, opened in November 1967. Many units were taken by chain stores such as Timpsons and Halfords, most of whom had not been represented in the town before. Only Marsh and Baxter, from Hagley Street, and the Midlands Gas Board and Wrenson's, from High Street, moved into the Precinct.

150 *Architect's impression of The Precinct and proposed flats, c.1965.*

The 10-storey block of flats which was to have soared above the shops was never built, but its place was taken by the new Central Library, which was built on seven floors. It too was designed by Bernard Engle and Partners, and built by John Laing Construction Ltd. The building was leased back to the Council for 99 years by the lessees of the shopping centre, Ravenseft Properties Ltd. The Council had the option to buy out this lease at any time before 1986.[4] The Library included a children's library, adult lending library, music and record library, a reference library, a 150-seat theatre and a coffee bar. It was opened on 11 November 1971 by Sir George Chandler, then president of the Library Association, who, damning with faint praise, remarked that it was one of the best-sited libraries that he had seen.

151 *The Precinct and new library, 1971.*

152   *The Cornbow Centre, 1989.*

In the late 1960s, all the shops on the west side of High Street were demolished and replaced by utilitarian shop units with concrete canopies overhanging the pedestrianised street; the same process transformed the south side of Peckingham Street between 1967 and 1969. Many long-established shops went out of business at this time, but Dancers Ltd, the outfitters, retained their old site, moving to the old Co-operative drapery shop in the Bull Ring in 1967, whilst their premises on the corner of Peckingham Street were rebuilt. The town centre was made traffic-free in 1968. Some sign of regret at the passing of the old townscape was expressed in 1975, when a petition signed by 1,000 people saved the *Lyttelton Arms*, High Street, from demolition. Local opposition did not, however, save the old library and Council Chamber on Hagley Street from demolition in 1978. It was replaced by another shopping complex, including a Presto supermarket, a W.H. Smith, a multi-storey car park and the Cornbow Hall, which opened in 1980.

Despite its bare concrete and unloved appearance, the Precinct served as Halesowen's principal shopping area for 20 years before it, too, was thoroughly rebuilt in 1988. The architects for the refurbishment were Seymour Harris Partnership, and the £5million project was executed by Bryant Construction. The main walkway was roofed over with double-glazed tinted glass panels, supported on A-shaped steel roof trusses that rested on the original concrete canopies. At the Hagley Street entrance two ornamental pyramids, each raised on four steel columns, flanked the automatic doors. At the Queensway end, the old restaurant and its concrete pedestal were removed. A glass roof was raised high above the square on four sets of three tubular steel columns. This created an atrium within the building, enabling a street café to be laid out on the lower floor. Access between the two shopping levels was made easier by the installation of new lifts and escalators. The Precinct remained open throughout the building work, with any construction which might endanger shoppers carried out overnight. The whole complex, renamed the 'Cornbow Centre', was officially reopened on 25 November 1989 to almost universal acclaim. Fifteen years later, the centre still compares well with most English shopping malls.

Notes

⌘⌘⌘

Abbreviations

B.C.A-Birmingham City Archives
D.A-Dudley Archives
H.R.O-Herefordshire Record Office
P.R.O-Public Record Office
S.R.O-Shropshire Record Office
W.R.O-Worcestershire Record Office

Chapter 1: Landlords and Tenants

1. Lyttelton, Charles, *Parochial Antiquities or Topographical Survey of Hagley, Frankley, Churchill, Clent, Arley and Halesowen*, Mss., Society of Antiquaries, London, p.133.
2. Lyttelton of Hagley Hall Collection, B.C.A. Mss. 3279.
3. Wilson, Rowland Alwyn (ed.), *Court Rolls of the Manor of Hales*, Part 3, 1933, p.179.
4. Amphlett, John (ed.), *Court Rolls of the Manor of Hales, Parts 1-2*, 1912, p.103.
5. *Ibid.*, p.136.
6. *Ibid.*, p.241.
7. H.R.O. E/12/VI/KBc9.
8. W.R.O. 2422/19 i.
9. B.C.A. 576597.
10. Razi, Zvi, *Life, Marriage and Death in a Midland Parish: economy, society and demography in Halesowen 1270-1400*, 1980, p.99.
11. B.C.A. 347156; Homans, G.C., *English Villagers of the 13th century*, p.283.
12. B.C.A. 346823; Field, R.K., *The Worcestershire Peasantry in the Later Middle Ages*, 1962, p.76.
13. B.C.A. 346847; Field, R.K., *op. cit.*, p.76.
14. Nash, T.R., *Collections for the History of Worcestershire*, 1799, Appendix p.xxvi.
15. *Ibid.*, p.xxvii.
16. B.C.A. 351877; Somers, F. and Somers, K.M., *Halas, Hales, Halesowen*, 1932, Appendix p.iii.
17. W.R.O. 4000/289 ii.
18. Prattinton Mss., Society of Antiquaries, Vol. 16, p.38.
19. B.C.A. 351841.
20. W.R.O. 4600/507.
21. W.R.O. 2422/30.
22. D.A. 8658 Bundle 14.

Chapter 2: Ironmasters and Nail-makers

1. Amphlett, John (ed.), *Court Rolls of the Manor of Hales, Parts 1-2*, 1912, p.566.
2. Nash, T.R., *Collections for the History of Worcestershire*, 1799, p.509.
3. B.C.A. 346233; Field, R.K., The Worcestershire Peasantry in the Later Middle Ages, 1962, p.152.
4. B.C.A. 347146; Nash, op. cit., Appendix p.xxxv.
5. B.C.A. 351958; Schubert, H.R., *History of the British iron and steel industry*, 1957, p.181.
6. Worcestershire Historical Society New Series Vol. 16, *Inventories of Worcestershire landed gentry 1537-1786*, p.96.

7. B.C.A. 351727.

8. Roy, Ian (ed.), 'Royalist ordnance papers 1642-46', *Oxfordshire Record Society*, Vol. 49, 1975, p.428.

9. H.R.O. E12/VI/Kac/29.

10. D.A. D/DE/IV Box 4, Bundle 9; Schubert, *op. cit.*, p.372.

11. H.R.O. E12/VI/KBc/7.

12. H.R.O. E/12/VI/KAc/40.

13. Schafer, R.G., 'A selection from the records of Philip Foley's Stour Valley Iron Works', Part 1, *Worcestershire Historical Society*, New Series Vol. 9, 1978, pp.40-3.

14. H.R.O. E12/VI/KBc/7.

15. Schafer, R.G., 'A selection from the records of Philip Foley's Stour Valley Iron Works', Part 2, *Worcestershire Historical Society*, New Series Vol. 13, 1990, pp.15-21.

16. *Ibid.*, p.39.

17. H.R.O. E/12/VI/Def/1; Johnson, B.L.C., 'The Foley partnerships: the iron industry at the end of the charcoal era', *Economic History Review*, 1952, p.326.

18. H.R.O. E12/VI/DEc/11.

19. Knight Mss. Formerly at Kidderminster Library, now W.R.O. 10470.

20. W.R.O. 10470 Box 72.

21. W.R.O. 8249.

22. W.R.O. 5467/76.

23. D.A. D/DE/IV Box 4, Bundle 9.

24. D.A. D/DE/IV Box 5, Bundle 7; Ball, Johnson, *William Caslon, Master of Letters*, 1973, p.48.

25. D.A. D/DE/IV Box 15, Bundle 8.

26. H.R.O. E/12/VI/KBc9.

27. W.R.O. 4600/870 vi.

28. W.R.O. 5467/98.

29. W.R.O. 5467/107.

30. W.R.O. 10470 Box 72.

31. Williams, Marjorie (ed.), *The letters of William Shenstone*, 1939, p.628.

32. W.R.O. 4600/870 vi.

33. W.R.O. 5467/98.

34. B.C.A. 605894.

35. W.R.O. 4600/49.

36. Lot 14 in sale, 20 June 1827.

37. D.A. 8658 Bundle 3.

38. B.C.A. 346314; Field, *op. cit.*, p.152.

39. B.C.A. 347162; Field, *op. cit.*, p.207.

40. H.R.O. E/12/VI/KBc9.

41. *Black Country Bugle*, 5 February 2004.

42. W.R.O. 5467/107.

43. W.R.O. 4600/49.

44. W.R.O. 4600/507.

45. Charity Commissioners, *Appendix to Further Report of the Commissioners for Inquiring Concerning Charities, County of Salop*, 1839, p.213.

46. Halesowen Gas Company, Centenary booklet, 1936.

47. W.R.O. 9941/1.

48. Children's Employment Commission, 1863, p.138.

49. Grove, C.F., 'A history of the button trade in Halesowen', *The Blackcountryman*, Vol. 17, 1984, no. 1, pp.36-40, no. 2, pp.6-10, no. 3, pp.23-25.

Chapter 3: Shops and Shopkeepers

1. B.C.A. 346717.

2. B.C.A. 346734.

3. B.C.A. 346736.

4. B.C.A. 346455.

5. B.C.A. 346468.

6. Somers, Frank (ed.), *Halesowen Churchwardens' Accounts* 1487-1582, 1952-7, p.80.
7. Nash, T.R., *Collections for the History of Worcestershire*, 1799, Appendix p.xxvi.
8. D.A. 8658/16.
9. Jones, N.H., *Walter Hall the Hygienic Barber (and others)*, 1994, p.33.
10. Rate book, W.R.O. 5243.
11. D.A. 8658/3.
12. W.R.O. 4906/2.
13. W.R.O. 4906/4 iv.
14. D.A. Z/233.
15. W.R.O. 2723.
16. B.C.A. 462/8.
17. W.R.O. 9941/1.
18. D.A. Z 198/1.
19. D.A. 8658 bundle 4.
20. D.A. 8658 bundle 5.
21. D.A. 8658 bundle 5.
22. B.C.A. 297264.
23. D.A. 8568 bundle 16.
24. W.R.O. 5491.
25. D.A. 8658 bundle 6.
26. W.R.O. 6487.
27. D.A. 8907.
28. W.R.O. 4906/7.
29. W.R.O. 4906/13.
30. W.R.O. 4906/12.
31. W.R.O. 9941/1.

Chapter 4: Pubs and Publicans
1. B.C.A. 347146.
2. W.R.O. 4000/289 ii.
3. W.R.O. 5491.
4. S.R.O. QE 2/1/2.
5. B.C.A. 297252.
6. B.C.A. 297254.
7. S.R.O. QE 2/1/6.
8. W.R.O. 4906/13.
9. W.R.O. 4906/7.
10. *Halesowen Who's Who*, 1951, pp.149-53.

Chapter 5: Roads, Canals and Railways
1. Williams, Marjories (ed.), *The letters of William Shenstone*, 1939, p.358.
2. B.C.A. 326646.
3. B.C.A. 288224.
4. Aris' *Birmingham Gazette*, 30 Jan 1797.

Chapter 6: Gentlemen's Houses
1. W.R.O. 2422/19.
2. Prattinton Mss., Society of Antiquaries, Vol.16 p.42.
3. Surrey History Centre BR/OC/1/12.
4. B.C.A. 442398-9.
5. Grazebrook, H. Sydney, *Heraldry of Worcestershire*, 1873, p.684.
6. Somers, F. and Somers, K.M., *Halas, Hales, Halesowen*, 1932 p.64.
7. Guildhall Library 11936/274/412962.
8. D.A. 8658 bundle 14.
9. Staffordshire Record Office D 695/1/12/74.
10. B.C.A. 390716.

11. Guildhall Library 11936/322/495993.
12. Sidwell, George, *Walter Somers Ltd – Times Remembered*, 1989, p.3.
13. W.R.O. 919/2.
14. W.R.O. 919/2; 2723/10.
15. D.A. 8658 bundle 10.
16. W.R.O. 4906/13.
17. Will of Joseph Coley of Drew's Forge, 1802.
18. W.R.O. 4906/3; Grazebrook, *op. cit.*, pp.272, 293.

Chapter 7: Churches and Chapels

1. Somers, F. (ed.), *Halesowen Churchwardens' Accounts*, Parts 1-3, 1952-5, p.95.
2. Ibid., p.104.
3. Mathews, A.G., Calamy Revised, 1934, p.383.
4. D.A. 8561: Plans of reinstatement of the Parish Church of Halesowen by Francis Goodwin.
5. Hone, the Rev. Richard Brindley, 'St John the Baptist Church, Halesowen', in *Proceedings of the Worcester Diocesan Architectural and Archaeological Society*, 1877.
6. Aitken, John (ed.), 'Census of Religious Worship 1851: the returns for Worcestershire', *Worcestershire Historical Society*, New Series Vol. 17, 2000, p.12.
7. Report of the Restoration Committee 1873-1885. D.A.8561.
8. Jones, D.H., *Halesowen Congregational Church 1807-1957*, 1957, p.10.
9. *Zion Methodist Chapel, Halesowen, Centenary Memoirs, 1842-1942*, 1942, p.4.
10. Halesowen Methodist Church, Birmingham Street, *The Birmingham Street Story 1868- 1968*, 1968, p.18.

Chapter 8: Schools and Schoolmasters

1. Charity Commissioners, Further Report of the Commissioners for Inquiring Concerning Charities, County of Salop, 1839, p.189.
2. W.RO. 2729/1 Item 51.
3. D.A. Z 134/1.
4. Jones, N.H., *The Islington Ragged School and its Founder, Caleb Bloomer*, 1987, p.14.
5. *Halesowen Tenter Street County Primary School Commemoration 1909-1959*, 1959, p.13.
6. *Halesowen Technical School, Halesowen College of Further Education, 1939-1960*, p.11.

Chapter 9: Local Government

1. *Halesowen's 21st Charter Anniversary Handbook, 1936-1957*, p.61.
2. Somers, F. (ed), *Halesowen Churchwardens' Accounts*, parts 1-3, 1952-5, p.80.
3. P.R.O. Exchequer Depositions, Shropshire, Easter 31 Chas I No. 15.
4. Nash, T.R., *Collections for the History of Worcestershire*, 1799, p.516.
5. W.R.O. 2723/4.
6. D.A., Halesowen Rural District Council Minutes,13 June 1900.
7. *Borough of Halesowen Charter Souvenir*, 1936.
8. Borough of Halesowen, *Record of Achievement of the Borough And County Councils*, 1972.

Chapter 10: The Re-development of Halesowen

1. D.A. Halesowen Borough Council Schedule of Deeds.
2. D.A. 8658 bundle 7.
3. D.A. Halesowen Borough Council Schedule of Deeds.
4. Borough of Halesowen *Last Will and Testament*, 1 February 1974.

BIBLIOGRAPHY

ঔৰ্ড

Amphlett, John (ed.), *Court rolls of the Manor of Hales, 1270-1307, Parts 1-2*, 1912

Amphlett, John, *A Short History of Clent*, 1890

Asquith, Betty, *The Lytteltons, a Family Chronicle of the nineteenth century*, 1975

Ball, Johnson, *William Caslon, Master of Letters*, 1973

Billingham, John, *The Earls High School, 1652-2000*, 2000

Billingham, John, *Geography around us: Halesowen*, 1998

Billingham, John, *History around us: Halesowen*, 1992

Blunt, Reginald, *Thomas Lord Lyttelton, the portrait of a rake, with a brief memoir of his sister, Lucy Lady Valentia*, 1936

Bradley, M. and Blunt, B., *History of Cradley Churches, Parts 1-3*,1998-9

Bradley, M. and Blunt, B., *History of Cradley: Wills and Inventories, a study of life in Cradley in the 16th and 17th centuries*, 2003

Brittain, W., *The Birmingham Street Story, 1868-1968*, 1968

Burns, Nancie, *Family Tree, an adventure in genealogy*, 1962

Chapman, N.A., *A History of Coal Mining around Halesowen*, 1999

Charity Commissioners, *Further Report of the Commissioners for Inquiring Concerning Charities, County of Salop*, 1839

Children's Employment Commission, 3rd Report, 1864, pp.135-8

Collins, Paul, *Black Country Canals*, 2001

Crew, Kathleen, *Life at Halesowen Abbey*, 1984

Crew, Kathleen, *The Medieval Manor of Halesowen 1293-1307*, 1988

Davenport, James, *The Grove Family of Halesowen*, 1912

Downing, Harcourt H., *The Nailmakers*, 2000

Eades, David L., *The Magistracy in Halesowen, c.1830-1997*, 1997

Eades, David L., *Halesowen*, 1998

Eades, David L., *Halesowen, a second selection*, 2000

Field, R.K., 'The Worcestershire Peasantry in the Later Middle Ages', University of Birmingham MA thesis, 1962

Flint, D.C., 'Industrial Inertia in Halesowen 1700-1918', University of Birmingham thesis, 1975

Gale, W.K.V., *Walter Somers Ltd, a history: 1866-1986*, 1987

Gregory, Kenneth, *History of Halesowen, an introduction to the sources*, n.d.

Hackman, F.W., *Oldbury and Round About*, 1915

Hadfield, Charles, *Canals of the West Midlands*, 1966

Hale, Michael and Williams, Ned, *By rail to Halesowen*, 1974

Halesowen Borough Council, *Halesowen Who's Who and Directory*, 1951

Halesowen Chamber of Trade, *Official Handbook 1922-3*, 1922

Harris, William, *History and Antiquities of the Borough and Parish of Halesowen*, 1831

Hazlehurst, Bill, *Sketches of Halesowen*, Vols 1-3, 1993-9

Hilton, R.H., *Medieval Society, the West Midlands at the end of the thirteenth century*, 1966

Hilton, R.H. 'Peasant movements in England before 1381', in *Essays in economic history*, Carus Wilson, E.M. (ed.), Vol. 2, 1962

Homans, G.C., *English Villagers of the Thirteenth Century*, 1970

Hunt, Joe, *History of Halesowen Abbey*, rev. ed., 1995

Hunt, Joe and Hunt, Julian, *Romsley and Hunnington, a millennium history*, 1999

Ince, Laurence, *The Knight Family and the British Iron Industry, 1695-1902*, 1991

Jeaves, Isaac Herbert, *Descriptive Catalogue of the Charters and Muniments of the Lyttelton Family*, 1893

Johnson, B.L.C., 'The Foley partnerships: the iron industry at the end of the charcoal era', *Economic History Review*, N.S. xvii, 1952

Johnson, B.L.C., 'The Stour Valley iron industry in the late seventeenth century', *Transactions of the Worcestershire Archaeological Society*, Series 2, iv, no. 3, 1950

Jones, D.H., *Halesowen Congregational Church, 1907-1957*, 1957

Lay, W.E., *Halesowen Parish Church St John Baptist*, 3rd edn, 1970

Lyttelton, Charles, *Parochial Antiquities or Topographical Survey of Hagley, Frankley, Churchill, Clent, Arley and Halesowen*, Mss., Society of Antiquaries, London

Nash, T.R., *Collections for the History of Worcestershire*, 2nd edn, 2 vols, 1799

Perry, Nigel, *A History of Stourbridge*, 2001

Raybould, T.J., *The Economic Emergence of the Black Country, a study of the Dudley estate*, 1973

Razi, Zvi, *Life, Marriage and Death in a Midland Parish, economy, society and demography in Halesowen 1270-1400*, 1980

Razi, Zvi, 'The Peasants of Halesowen 1270-1400, a demographic, social and economic study', University of Birmingham PhD thesis, 1976

Schafer, R.G. (ed.), *A Selection from the Records of Philip Foley's Stour Valley Iron Works, Parts 1-2*, 1978-90

Schubert, H.R., *History of the British Iron and Steel Industry from c.450 B.C. to A.D. 1775*, 1957

Schwarz, Lena, *The Halesowen Story*, 1955

Sidwell, Graham, *Walter Somers Ltd – times remembered*, 1989

Somers, F. (ed.), *Halesowen Churchwardens' Accounts, Parts 1-3*, 1952-5

Somers, F. and Somers, K.M., *Halas, Hales, Halesowen*, 1932

Sotheby Parke Bernet & Co., *Catalogue of the Lyttelton Papers*, 1978

Williams, Marjorie (ed.), *The Letters of William Shenstone*, 1939

Williams, Marjorie, *William Shenstone, a chapter in eighteenth century taste*, 1935

Williams, Ned, *Cinemas of the Black Country*, 1982

Williams, Ned, *The Co-op in Birmingham and the Black Country*, 1993

Willis-Bund, J.W. (ed.), *Victoria History of the County of Worcester*, 4 vols, 1901-24

Wilson, H.R., *David Parkes, 1763-1833*, 1979

Wilson, Rowland Alwyn, *Court rolls of the Manor of Hales, Part 3, containing additional courts of the years 1276-1301 and Romsley Courts, 1280-1303*, 1933

Wyndham, Maud, *Chronicles of the 18th Century, founded on the correspondence of Sir Thomas Lyttelton and his family*, 1924

INDEX

Page numbers in **bold** refer to illustrations

175

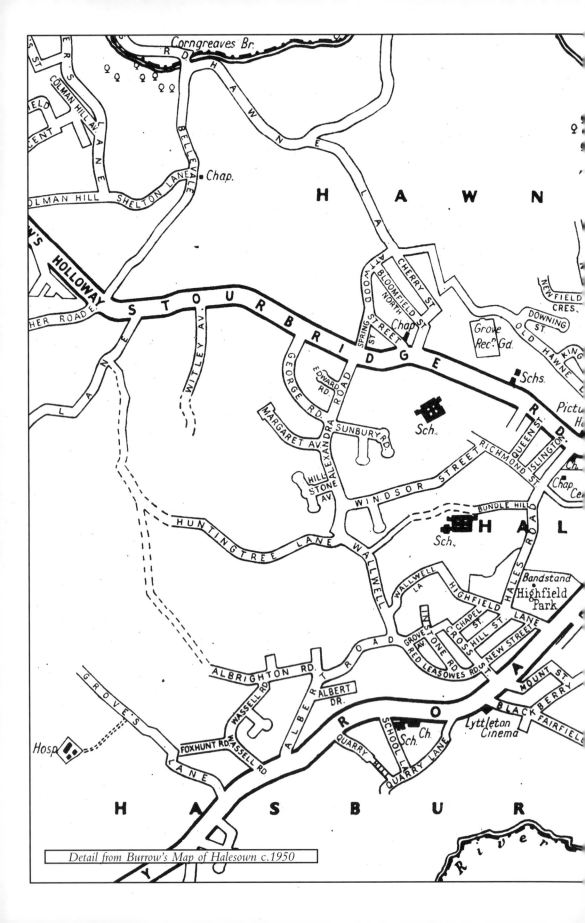

Detail from Burrow's Map of Halesown c.1950